The first issue of Geny's Sequel "92 Years Of Love" is to raise funds for Veterans charities, as witnessed by:

—Susan Gasiewicz and Kim Longo:

The Stars & Stripes Classic have had the honor of receiving donations from Geny Heywood to benefit our efforts in helping our Veteran community. Ms. Heywood's past donations were critical in assisting the Gold Star Mothers Food Pantry and providing meals to Veterans in need & also to purchase supplies for an Agriculture Program to teach Veterans to grow their own food & raise their own livestock to be self sufficient. With her financial assistance, we are able to send packages to deployed soldiers over the past few years & provide/train Service Dogs for PTSD Veterans upon their return from battle.

—-Jeff Wells:

I have known Geny Heywood for the past ten years, and I can say without a doubt, Geny is one of the most amazing people I've ever met. Her youthful energy, stamina, and many talents are the envy of us all! Over the years, Geny has accomplished many different activities that have raised thousands of dollars to assist military families through WISH for OUR HEROES, a charity that I founded in 2009. Through her hard work, Geny has assisted dozens of military families with basic needs such as food, shelter, transportation, child needs, and medical expenses. Thank you, Geny, for all that you do for our heroes. To learn more about WISH for OUR HEROES, visit www.wishforourheroes.org

NINETY TWO YEARS
L*of*OVE
Witnessings of an Old Lady
THE SEQUEL

GENY HEYWOOD

XULON PRESS

Xulon Press
2301 Lucien Way #415
Maitland, FL 32751
407.339.4217
www.xulonpress.com

Paperback ISBN-13: 978-1-6628-4164-4
Ebook ISBN-13: 978-1-6628-4165-1

Table of Contents

Forward. vii

La Sage-Femme. 1

Memories of Youth 5

Learning Crafts. 9

Our Refugees of 1939
       (and the Vendean Genocide of years before). 17

In the Favelas. 25

Home again, 1982 49

Forward

A friend of mine once pointed out that it was much better to say: *"Remember"* than to use the words "Do not forget". So please, *remember,* I have lived many years of our human history that many of you especially, you the very young people, did not.

If I were to leave this planet today, nobody else could tell you what really has happened starting in 1930 and up to the day when **you** were born. I know that you have and shall have in olden days, your very own history to recall but it is newsworthy for you to also learn about other peoples' lives. Yes I meant plural, peoples of the world.

At the conclusion of this, my final book of Memoirs that I write for my descendants and for readers who might be interested, I will include some fascinated facts of the past years that your own life story might not reckon. Trust me, the details of the past that my forever friends are reciting for you to read are absolutely priceless. This is why I want you to learn about those great extra details.

Remember also that in later years, you too should tell your descendants about what you are living and experiencing today because they, your posterity, will not know about it unless you *remember* to tell them, your own descendants.

One day might come when you cannot recall what you did in such or such year. Or even a week before. Your gray matter might fail you one day. I hope not, but it could happen.

You probably already know that you could spend a fortune on expert advise to counsel you on how to keep your memory rather healthy for your entire life. It might very well work, but, it might not.

Would you believe that I can tell you how you might very well *prevent* such loss of memory to happen to you. I am right now going to tell you how my system helped me. Maybe you will be able to try it and it might very well help you also. Let me try to explain my very simple method for absolutely no fee, counsel totally free of charge?

A life in the nineteen thirties and those many years I have faced since, have probably been very different from the sort of experiences that, you all, my descendants and interested readers, have lived so far and might have to face in the future.

Being able to recollect the past, or just being confident to simply remember, should be an exclusive right available to every human being, especially as they age. Unfortunately it is not always true. It hurts my soul, it bothers me so much when I meet people of my generation who cannot recall anything of what happened to them or to their loved ones, in their many past years of existence. Sometimes, they even forget what happened to them yesterday.

Why should the brain so often wants to draw a blank on memorable facts of our past life? This is such a mystery. It is a worry of mine, yes, since at times, I think I am reaching that stage when my children tell me that I already told them the same story at least three times.

Why should our brain wants to erase some of our past? Why should our inner head forget something important. Our bygone days represent not just our own yore, it is a chronicle of a past time that our young people of today cannot imagine and yet, might want to know, to learn and to hear about. Our young ones were not witness to those past events, we were. Our past is HISTORY, but of course, it is only past chronicle if we can remember it.

My, now late brother Michel, almost five years my senior, said to me one day: "How can you remember all those long ago days? I have no idea what you are talking about..." This happened when I was seventy and he, almost seventy five. Now, his son Philippe, a recently retired journalist, often asks me questions about his parents' life. Frequently I can remember and most of the time, I am able to give him the detailed answers that his father could not.

I believe that I might have most of the solution to a mystery that could help you, yes you and so many other people. To be able to remember your past as you are getting on in years, you must start making notes now and keep on doing it. Do not just take a recording on a cell phone, this is absolutely useless. It will not help you. Believe me it is futile.

Take a pen or a pencil (I always tried to use a pen) and jot down anything you think about. Facts that later on, you might want to recall, stories you never wanted to forget, details of many events, prices, news, dates, names...write them down. Put those notes away and pull out this recorded list often, correct it if necessary, add to it...write down something else, again, and again. I did that for years, and, I am still doing it.

Perhaps it sounds absurd to you but by doing so, keeping manual records while using your own hand and brain **to *write it down, and looking at it as often as required,*** I believe that your brain is using what I call the **VISUAL** memory. As you write it down on paper and see it, you do not realize that it files details in your gray matter much more efficiently than you cellphone memory could, and you brain immediately files it there, in one of your *human data filing cabinet* forever. Believe me it works. Even if it delays just partially your potential memory loss, it is well worth the trial.

Because of the interest shown in my recently published Memoirs, " 91 Years Of Love, Witnessings Of An Old Lady", I feel that perhaps I should keep on telling about the numerous facts that make my life's history such an Odyssey. Well, it does, at least to me, while I can still remember what happened in those past years, it makes me feel well.

You actually might find some of those stories interesting. Those many past times, the many years, weeks and months of my life presented such different times from what we live today! Here now my friends is **The Sequel.** A lifespan of almost a century includes many events. Here is the first one. It is a story I would like to share with you since it has been sort of bothering me for too many years.

LA SAGE-FEMME

*L*et us take a few moments to search our mind and try to open a mystery of a century ago that I have not yet solved. You might find that actually there is an answer to this post WW1 enigma that took place in my Vendean birth village of La Chataigneraie, located close to three hundred miles south of Paris.

At this stage, I must tell you the story I titled LA SAGE-FEMME, These french words translate as, The Wise Woman. It really means, *The midwife.* I would like for you to find a conclusion of your own to the narrative.

You did not yet hear me speak of Madame Quoiriet, my friend Jacques' mother. I mention my buddy Jacques in my story telling about the dancing soldiers, the German prisoners of war. As the famous WW2 singer of Britain, Vera Lynn said when she sang The White Cliffs Of Dover..."Just you wait and see".

This lady, Madame Quoirier was the rather busy midwife, our only village stork really, just a little older than my mother was. At the time, meaning when my brother was born in August nineteen twenty six, the two women were next door neighbors.

When the so-called wise woman had brought my brother into the world, then delivered Mom of my almost seven pound live carcass in nineteen thirty, the two women were not, just toiling neighbors, they sort of were on friendly terms, two busy ladies, occasionally sharing an idea or a gossip over a cup of chicory on the sidewalk in front of their homes.

But it was many years later that Mrs Q had related a rather intriguing story to my mother, who, then, had recounted it to me much later on, when I was a mother of four children. Secrets were well kept in those archaic days of our village life. They had to be.

It so happened that one summer evening, sitting on our house front steps, in great secrecy, the said midwife had told my mother about a mysterious event that had sort of affected her and now was going to affect and worry both women.

The inexplicable event had taken place in La Chataigneraie, already many years before. Mrs Q finally was clearing it off her chest by pulling it out in the open and sharing the burden from her soul.

This rather mysterious occurrence had happened when the sage-femme as a new bride in our village, had started her important carrier...she had to share her secret now, this minute, and my Mom was the confident.

Here goes the mystery:

The midwife was already asleep next to her husband after a very exhausting time on her medical calling of delivering babies. Suddenly, a laud banging on her front door had told her there was going to be no rest for her that late and dark night.

An unknown man was waiting at the door, a horse drawn cart was behind him on the street and in the darkness she could see another stranger, a man, sitting there in the cart, holding the reins of the horse. She was then asked to abide by a very secret mission.

They needed her services urgently the man closest to her said. He needed to cover her eyes and take her to a distant unknown location. She was asked to be tactful and to forget the involvement upon her return home. She was assured that she was going to be well paid for her troubles.

Grabbing her bag that was always waiting in the entrance of her residence's door, the rather panicked lady felt she had no choice but to accept the challenge. She sat between the two men on the hard bench of the horse cart and was blind folded by the man who had come to her door.

Being exhausted, she soon fell asleep between the two silent mysterious guides and sometime later, was awakened suddenly unaware of time and distance traveled. As the sleep wore off and she became aware of the ceased clip-clop of the horse hoofs, she was aware of a great silence. This announced to her, an arrival to a clandestine destination.

She was lifted down from the transport, still blind-folded and unsure of her footing, was then helped walking by the men holding her arms, one on each side of her. The two escorts then guided her to what she felt had to be a mansion or a castle or a huge house while she was directed to an entrance way.

She said to my mother that upon wakening, she could feel the cold air, she could hear the wind whispering through the trees and felt all around her like a swaying of plants and vegetation. She explained how she felt the crackling noise of gravel under her feet, and said she could definitely smell some forest vegetation. She thought she had arrived to what she believed could be, the grounds of a castle.

Since I, right now, today, can remember well the whole area of my birth village, I know there were several of those huge properties around that old part of the bocage. Today they are still there. Most have been transformed into retirement homes, B&B's or hotels.

When I recall that strange story, I cannot help but force my mind to figure out where that property might be located. Where, at which place, could the lady have been taken that night, about a hundred years ago.

So now here is our fully awake midwife, arrived on the secret stage of an unknown task prospect. While having just noticed such details that your instinct tells you to observe in moments of anxiety, and multiplied with feelings of insecurity, the lady is now led into what she believes to be a large hallway, then the noise of a door opening and she is now in a huge room where the black shawl covering her eyes is finally removed.

On a bed, is a young girl wearing a black mask, obviously in great need of the midwife's help. Nobody else around. Mrs Q notices that the tall windows of the room are draped to hide possible identity of a local.

She gets to work immediately. The two men are there watching silently and responding to every request of water and whatever is needed in the circumstances. No useless conversation, only the painful insistent moaning of the young mother-to-be is breaking the silence.

After having delivered the now very silent young new mother of a healthy baby boy, the midwife is immediately paid generously and is now returned home under the very same secret travel conditions, and again, with a black scarf over her eyes.

During the trip back home Mrs Q. stays awake, does no say a word. It is possible that the driver keeps on traveling rather fast now since the lady feels that some daylight starts to appear. The driver takes many turns and is trying to confuses the route. It could also be very possible that the newborn saw the light only a short distance away from the town or just on the edge of town, nobody will ever know.

Now, my concern today is still as it was when I first heard the narrative, a very strange and worried feeling concerning a child born some years before I came on this earth...
What really happened to that little boy?

MEMORIES OF YOUTH

Over the years, several of my friends on learning of my tormented life when I was under the tutelage of my father till age twenty one, have asked me why I did not just leave. What people might not understand is that a girl of my generation in France was supposed to stay under the tutelage of her father and in his home so that she would be supposedly *protected*. There was absolutely no way I could leave.

A girl could not just walk away, she would be searched for, found, arrested, and sent to a House of Correction. I heard this threat so many times that I came to visualize the place, it would be hell on earth most certainly; A snake pit. I had nightmares about the place so in my mind, the devil I knew was probably better than the one I did not know.

Many girls were not protected but were battered. I was not the only one. A drunk father would hit his children without mercy and since this was his right in a french law, nobody could do anything. It was the father's right to use any methods he liked in raising his children.

I remember some women of my neighborhood making fun of two young girls we knew, the daughters of a vegetable merchant who when they referred to their Dad, would say "our Darling Papa".

Without saying anything, I used to think:"I wish I could say the same, but I cannot" and I never told anyone yet but already as a young child, I had considered how I could dispose of the father who made my life so miserable.

My idea of leaving and immigrating to the north American continent took shape very early for me. I had heard about some people who shortly before WW2 were leaving to go to America. Later when I really learned geography, I realized how far I could go and never be beaten again. I would look at that map of the world and say to myself:"one day I will live there".

Looking back at my situation, today I wonder, since many people in my village knew I was battered, why didn't somebody help me? The police, the doctor, the priest? Nobody did anything and when I was sixteen and a neighbor saw me with a black eye, it was suggested I could get my emancipation, but it was easier said than done. How could I even learn the process? So I waited till the age of twenty one and left, went as far as I could, and did not return for nine years. For me, this had been the only way to solve my problem.

One day, just before the war, early in 1939, there was a meeting held in a back room at a restaurant of the village. All fathers had been asked to come and talk about Mr. Barbeau the teacher at the government boys' school who used to slap and beat his students. I must say that his wife was the teacher at the girls school and was beating her students too. I was one of her martyrs.

Any way, it happened that, one day, one of the bigger boys after getting a slap on the face from his teacher, the man Barbeau, the boy had turned around and given a slap to the teacher in return. That had made history and all the fathers were wondering on the steps to take but really feeling happy that one of their boys knew how to fend for himself. The father of the boy who had indeed defended himself had invited the other fathers, those of the whole group of school boys, to meet with him and decide of what step to take now and on the kind of decision they could make.

At the beginning of the meeting my father had stood up and declared:" Your boy deserved what he received and I am on the side of the teacher". Suddenly the father who wanted to protect his son at school had shouted to my father: "We order you right now to shut your trap

Engerbeau, and we do not want to hear your opinion. We all know how you raise your children with a stick and beat the shit out of them, so shut up!"

My father had left in a huff and never attended such meeting again. But at that get together, it had been finally evaluated that in the end, nothing could be done. Corporal punishment was the rule and that was that. I heard that story from my brother when we were already both old people. He had not forgotten that one!

I should mention here also: remember that this was my own and one family, it was the only one I had. Where could I go for help? And what nobody can really understand is that I was growing up during a war! The unknown, to me, appeared even more perilous than the life I knew.

Anyhow, let's forget about this subject now. I need to go back to my own history, the sequel to my Memoirs.

Here are a few stories that might be interesting to my readers but first I need to elaborate on my friends, the boys I knew. The midwife's son is the one with whom I shall start.

Madame Quoirier's son was Jacques, a boy just my age. We sort of discovered each other and became good friends when we danced together as teenagers after the war. He kissed me once and he tried to convince me that we could do very well together.

At about the same time, another boy by the same first name was my next door neighbor Jacques Delignet who told me the day after the war ended that he had loved me from the time we were very little while we had chatted a few times from our parents upstairs bedroom window.

There were a few boys my generation with whom I associated when groups of young people happened to meet at fairs or other get-togethers but of course all these, only after the war. Young people did not go from one friend to the other as they do now everywhere. People stayed close to their family. And, during WW2, we did not even sing, life was too sad. Everybody was much too worried. We the children could feel the tension, the suffering, the reactions to bad news. And, boys could be so easily grabbed by the gestapo and sent to work in Germany they had to watch their steps.

Even today, I noticed a few years ago how cautious the people of my village still were. When I stayed there for a while, I could see the old ways of hiding.

As soon as night falls, everybody lock themselves up, shutters pulled on windows and all doors and gates locked up. The streetlights are turned off at 11 pm. Sort of a remembering of war curfew.

With my secret ideas of immigrating in my youth, I could never have allowed myself to fall in love with the boys my generation, those from my village. All were wonderful kids, hardworking, intelligent, polite, none would ever have been rude to any of us girls.

Among us the young people, sex was never spoken about and I only know of one young couple who at age fifteen had become intimate. They were married right away with the approval of the parents on both side. It was said how the two kids had walked first in the office of city hall and then in the church, dressed simply and holding hands, They were married discretely with the parents on each side. Then the young couple had moved to another town where the young husband now had a job in his uncle's business and a very pregnant young bride was now keeping house for her man.

For me, having fallen in love with Jean Aumarchand when I was sixteen, could have been Heaven if he had married me. I loved his Mom, I loved his aunt, and I adored him, my very first love. I would have been many miles away from my parents since I would be in Dordogne, in the center of France. But since Jean made it clear that he would never marry, I could plan nothing in the way of a wedding with my first love. All that kept growing secretly in my mind was that dream of my immigration to America to make a better life for myself. So I made it, and have been happy on this land of the free. Thank you America The Beautiful!

LEARNING CRAFTS

*S*hortly after D-Day before my going to boarding school, it is now summer of 1944, I am almost fourteen years old. Somebody has loaned me a couple of paperback romance to read. I remember the title of the one: Aimee et laissee par son Legionnaire = Loved and abandoned by her Legionnaire. My father saw my reading material and decided that it was not the kind of literature that was suitable for me to have. But when I said they were on loan, he did not destroy them. I returned them to the compassionate lender, a lady I knew.

I must say that actually there was nothing wrong with this cheap reading material. You had to make it physically look like a finished small reading book yourself. It was printed as a huge full large sheet, then folded as many times as there were pages and stapled or sewn on the fold. The reader had to cut around the pages to open the now finished book. I had only read that one story titled above.

As it turned out, the Legionnaire story was very close to the situation that a friend of mine lived herself as a child. She, my friend Louise told me her very same many years ago past existence of 1965. We met in Houston and became friends while raising our children close to each other.

Her mother had been married to a legionnaire. They lived in Toulon then, in South of France. One day, worried about her husband not having returned after an assignment, mother felt she had to find him. The lady now although living under extremely poor french conditions, somehow managed to pack her two young children and take them to North Africa and search for Dad. Mekness was the place where the Legionnaire was supposed to have been last seen. WW2 started and this family ended up living in a Moroccan slum very miserably till long after the war.

Father was never located but by the time living conditions were finally improving, the mother and children had somehow survived. My friend Louise, at the time was working as a young cashier in a store. She met and married a wonderful US GI who saved them all. The Legionnaire's descendants are now like I am, happily living on the land of the free.

Now getting back to that pre-boarding school summer days of mine. After putting an end to my supposedly unsuitable romantic reading, my father took me to meet and speak with, Miss Anais. The lady's house was on the next street from our home, she made a living sewing for people but mostly doing mending of clothing. She had never done an apprenticeship as a certified dressmaker so legally she could not call herself a dressmaker, she was a mender.

Miss Anais, was an older spinster who had survived working this way for many years in the home that her parents had left her when she was still very young. They had departed from this earth taken away towards the end of the huge Flu epidemic, a pandemic that killed over fifty million people all over the world when she was probably eighteen or twenty years old.

People would bring work for Miss Anais like most village people did. Each community made sure everybody did some kind of work to be able to eat and pay their bills, even small invoices had to be managed. Taxes on homes and other properties, electricity if you were lucky to have paid to have it installed in your house in the 1930's. Of course people had to eat so they had to buy some items although many had a garden. They could not always grow everything in their small patch of garden so they had to purchase some food.

We made most of our clothing and other things last forever so somebody had to help mend them if within families, mothers and grandmothers had not enough time to repair and patch the wearable objects.

We had in our village two regular professional dressmakers for women and one only tailor for men. I remember my mother taking some old clothing from a trunk kept in our attic, those things had been sent to her by my financially better off godmother who had no children. Mom took some of those gift items to the dressmaker close to our house. Those old clothes but still very good, were to be remade in something for me to wear.

In our village there was a store where the lady, who owned the shop was a WW I widow. She sold material by the meter but my mother could not often afford to buy new material. In fact that business lady did not make much money from this commerce and her son, a bachelor who lived with her, stayed home and helped her pay the bills. He made a living telling fortunes.

He was a good counselor and people came from far to inquire some advise from him. My mother suggested I go talk to him the day before I left my father's house, one week before my twenty first birthday when I was going to England. So I did go for the teller to advise me, and guess what...The gentleman appeared to counsel me well in many ways. But why did he have to say that I would marry five times? Over the years I did, yes, I married five times and every time I did, I remembered the guy.

I felt that while telling my future, he had placed that idea in my mind that it was OK to do multiple marriages. What did he know, he never married.

Without realizing it at first, I know that he had pushed this to my inner thoughts. Since I feel he had planted that seed in my psyche, I will try to fool his memory now and try to get married once more :) a sixth time, that will teach him to review the mental demonstration while he is in heaven or where ever he happens to be!

Back to Miss Anais and the other dressmaker…Every time some clothing had to be made for me as I was growing up, I was always offered to select in a magazine what my new outfit should look like, so I would do that in great expectation. Then I would go several times to the dressmaker and she would pin here and pin there, chalk on a few places and the next and last time I would go with my mother to get it tried on me for the terminal creation checking. My Mom, having paid for the work, we would then bring my new outfit home.

I do not have to tell you I guess, my new attire never looked like the model I had chosen on the magazine. I was always very disappointed but what the heck, I had nothing better to wear anyway, so I did not complain.

Only once in my young life, actually I remember being very pleased. It was just after the war in 1945…winter, I was fifteen, my mother paid the dressmaker to make me a pair of warm long pants. European girls were never to be seen in those outfits before, only after the war. Remember I did not grow up in America!

After those great american movies of the late forties that we started to see in our village, our eyes were opened up. We the french women understood that the ladies on the USA continent could wear pants and get away with their ideas of freedom and liberty.

I guess the french women then accepted the challenge. They called the pants "pantalons de Plage" = beach pants. Yes you can smile! Beach Pantaloon should be worn by clowns right? Anyway.

So now here I had a pair of long warm pants. They were navy blue and made from some thin sort of woolly blanket but how wonderful they made me feel once I was wearing them. If you could only know how great my legs felt for the very first time in my life. I felt warm from my waistline to my feet. What a wonderful new feeling. This was the only pair of pants I had until I made some for myself later on when I could find a way to get some material, even if recycled.

Pants, slacks, bloomers, trousers, pantaloons, call them whatever you like, all I know is that my legs felt warm every winter after I left home. No more stockings that only went up a few inches above my knees and were held with elastic garters. Those hoses were always too short and my upper legs were always freezing in winter.

I should here explain about jobs, the work that people did in my village. Some ladies I knew survived doing ironing, laundry, mending, washing dishes, cleaning houses, looking after children, even nursing other mothers' babies after some poorer mothers had children of their own had milk to spare. Wet nurses they were called. We looked after our own people in Vendee, like multitudes did everywhere else in the so-called civilized European countries.

I heard my mother say to my father once: "If everybody did what those neighbors, the D's keep on doing, all our people trying to survive from the *Petits Metiers,* would starve. Why do they do everything themselves?" (Petits Metiers meant menial jobs).

It was everybody's responsibility, all the people, the entire community, had to make sure everyone worked. Even rather poor people like our family was, would employ and pay others to do most small jobs that our family could have done without their help.

One lady I knew plucked the feathers off chickens and since you would always buy two chickens at one time, from the market (an old law), and only for very special occasions, the plucking was sure to need extra accommodating fingers. And, the feathers pulling job better not tear the skin of the poultry either, you would not be hired for that job again!

I remember one old lady having tried to hide the mistake, she had used thread and a needle and had sewn the skin of the chicken back the best she could. She was only hired to do some washing or ironing for our family after that.

On that one previously mentioned day of my particular reading mentioned above, when my father had seen me studying what he considered useless literature, he took me with him to speak with Miss Anais. Would she please consider taking me as a free helper for at least this summer? He told her how all I wanted to do was read foolish romances. He added "but my daughter knows a lot about sewing". And, this is how I was hired right away.

As it turned out, then I was "employed" for the whole summer, and, for the other vacation times also. Absolutely no pay of course, not even a cup of tea, but Miss Anais found that since I could sew much better than she had expected, she was eager for me to help her. I also learnt in exchange, other sewing concepts from that lady's own skillfulness of many passed years practice. Next thing I knew, she had another girl working next to me. Miss Anais had suddenly figured out the performance benefits of what a commercial enterprise can bring.

When I was a small girl, it appears that every old lady I knew, and I watched all of them attentively while they were working, had, not always knowingly, taught me something with needles, threads and a thimble. Today I sincerely say thank you to those dear long departed souls. At age ten, I could already make beautiful button holes. I should also cite that there was a class of Good Home Keeping in all our elementary schools.

I must remark here that the painting and the drawing done by creative persons, the actual artists, were not really appreciated. That is why most noteworthy artists you now read and hear about, had a very hard time surviving.

Something you might not realize nowadays is that in my young years, even small children were expected to learn activities like sewing and knitting. We did not depend on trade and other people to make everything for us, we made many items by ourselves. But to paint and draw was certainly not encouraged as I so want to promote the arts with the craft to this day.

I so well remember Madame Soucher, the wife of the Garage owner, she was already middle age, had no children and one day, she spent a couple of hours with me sitting in front of her house, making a simple slip for a doll. I learnt different ways of sewing with her on that day and I was very pleased.

My mother had shown me how to draw a violet once and that was it... she could have shown me more, I knew she could have, no, to her that was wasted time. An older girl one day showed me how she could draw a ballerina. Oh what beautiful picture she made...I tried it often after that. Mine was never as beautiful as the ballet dancer the young lady had drawn.

I guaranty that the time you spend showing children a craft that you know and they do not, is a time very well spent on your part. Please consider doing this for a child. He or she will never forget you. I remember the day a lady showed me how to burn a bird picture on a piece of wood. Problem was I burnt my fingers and refused to do it any more. I was probably eight years old. I had enjoyed only the first part of the lesson, the drawing part, very much.

My dear late husband Leonard Reed who gave up his battle with cancer four years ago, told me an interesting story while at the end of his life he was lying in his bed reminiscing. When he was in his second year of school in Lompoc California, a young teacher who happened to be from Hawaii, insisted on teaching all the children, boys and girls students of her class, how to knit. Len said, "she was so cute, so beautiful, and, so patient, we all loved our young teacher. We all learnt to knit".

So, please show children something artistic you can do and ask those young persons to show it to others. Let the young people learn something useful, something intelligent. ***Those children will never forget you.***

Before I leave this story, let me tell you a few items that might interest you about the thirties:

— The zipper was invented because buttons were too expensive
— One famous phrase was "Brother, can you spare a dime?"

— People in the US trying to fight the dust Bowl had to move away from their houses.
— The US family income was less than $2,000.00 but in Europe way below that
— Scotch tape was invented by 3M
— Bakeries started slicing the bread and also selling buns and other goods
— The FBI was chasing gangsters to get the tax money they never wanted to pay
— Chocolate chips are invented and children love them
— Franklin Roosevelt starts thinking about The New Deal
— Mickey Mouse is invented and becomes very popular
— Nickels are not yet minted
— Some people in America live in cardboard homes.

The stock market actually started to recover only the year I arrived on this continent in 1954. You might think it was before that but no, it was not.

These are the kinds of written records, the notes I often still write down with a pen on pieces of paper to file inside my brain. I know it sounds silly but I am sure that it helps my memory.

OUR REFUGEES of 1939

(AND THE VENDEAN GENOCIDE OF YEARS BEFORE)

*I*n my memoirs, I speak of the people we had welcomed in our village when the German army was entering France through the Ardennes. You can see the picture I included. My smiling mother is trying her best to convince Madame Triolet and her four children that they and other refugees are going to be all right in our village. The poor sad mother and her children were in great despair, you can understand it well by looking at their gloomy facial expressions on that photograph.

Although none of us hosts were showing fear in front of those expatriates, we all knew that in a short time, we too were going to be invaded by those very same enemy soldiers they had ran away from. These armies would be at our own doors any day now as well. And of course this is exactly what really happened.

A few weeks before such a great sudden confusion of a war declaration had occurred, and before our very own armies were rushed to the front then defeated in the northern part, the French government had actually tried to set up a quick plan. They figured somebody had to make, to organize a program for the very near approaching dreaded situation that many people could predict, meaning our unavoidable total invasion.

It was determined by the French government that these refugees, these people, running away from their Ardennes homes, would be sort of directed as safely as possible, somewhere...but where?

Vendee, my own birthplace, had been the very first credible place suggested on the politicians list. It appeared to be an acknowledged manageable area. It was believed that the crowds of moving Ardennes people could be semi-protected somewhat safely if directed towards our land, just South of that Brittany head you can see on a map. The reason was probably because of our being such a poorer part of France, we were really not that much overpopulated and because of this, we had plenty of available room in our small towns and villages.

Earlier, in that summer of 1939, as a sort of precaution, the hospitals and orphanages on the German border, had already been emptied of their contents. The older patients, the handicapped people, and every last one of those mental patients kept under hospital control, all those vulnerable human beings as well as all the orphans, had to be protected and moved very fast. So this is why they were evacuated early and placed into many distant hospitals and other available places.

All hospitals and homes like the preventoriums, were, right away, completely filled up everywhere and as far away as possible as they could be placed from the German border.

A preventorium was actually a very well organized camp where children were kept while their parents were sick. Many were originally started by the church and ran by the Catholic nuns. I was kept at my grandparents' home for months at a time when my father was very ill with tuberculosis, but my only sibling, my brother Michel, was living with other children in one of those preventoriums on the sea shore, in Longeville.

Somebody in the French government of 1939 must have figured out that mental patients were going to be soon the first to be in a very great danger if found by the invaders. It appears that these special people's lives were in peril, so that is the reason they were the very first patients to be relocated by the French government.

Now try to think of what Hitler ordered to do to these people, to all these mental patients later on. If their families had not managed to keep them in hiding somewhere in their attics or tool sheds in back gardens, they all ended up murdered and burnt.

I remember an older gentleman, a mental patient of my village whose widowed sister Madame Durer, kept him hidden in what appeared to be her old abandoned house. There was a huge wooden gate at the entrance of her walled living quarters. She lived actually right in the center of town, she had no children. She was a WW1 widow. Her gate was always locked and nobody really knew anything about this residence. Somehow, the occupying troupes never bothered with the house hidden behind those old walls and wooden gate. They may have searched it at the start and found the property not at all suitable for the soldiers of occupation.

Because as a child I was wondering what mystery was hidden behind those boards, I had noticed a small crack in the gate and I would look in the hidden secret yard on my way to school. I could never see any-body. One morning suddenly I peaked inside and two eyes were staring back at me so I got scared, ran away and never looked again. I feel a chill in my spine right now remembering how frightened I was. I ran down that street to the school and never said anything to anyone...but I never dared to be a *voyeuse* and look again.

But back to the large number of the refugees, these people we wel-comed in our rather miserable Vendee in 1939. I just checked since now I know that records have been kept and can be looked at in all these public opened files. It was eighty two thousand refugees from Ardennes who ended up on this, our own small part of French soil.

Later on, with a permit that had to be approved by and also granted by the invading authorities, some of these Northern people who were very homesick, wanted to return home. So a few thousands Ardennes citi-zens, now and then would find their way back to their mostly destroyed houses. They would try to live there the best they could. I remember a lady telling my mother in front of me later, why she had returned to our village, she had absolutely nothing left of her house in the Ardennes. Why I remember this, most likely is because the lady had said:" all I found was the chamber pot on a pile of stones of my totally destroyed home". Of course I would note and recall such detail as a child. I could visualize the chamber pot that we all had under our beds, sitting on a pile of stones, among the ruins of her town.

By the end of WW2, only six thousand refugees of this welcomed exiled multitude, had remained. I know that our small town had sheltered several families, six groups I believe, mostly of course, mothers and children with often a few very old men. They were the Ardennes refugee people who came first, and most of those people had remained in our village for the entire duration of the war.

My godfather Camille for instance (see that wedding photo at the end of my memoirs) had married a sweet young lady, Gisele, a girl from the Ardennes who had suddenly appeared with her sister, in his village near Chantonnay. Of course, she stayed with her family for the rest of her life in Vendee and died there. Gisele is buried in that village with her husband, their third child, a son who died young, and all of Camille's relatives including his grandparents, who happen to be my very own great grandparents Petit, my Mom's maternal grandparents.

I did meet again two of my refugee friends, Michelle and Jacques Triolet (from that picture, they are the two kids on the left), once after the war. They suddenly found me and surprised me in 1953. They stayed with me forty-eight hours. I was not much of a hostess, no money to spare, only little food. I had only a small rented room for the six months that I worked at the American PX in La Rochelle.

The strangest thing was that although we had been so close for four years during the war and even after, by correspondence, now we had actually very little in common as grownups when we met.

We used to write to each other once in a while, yet after that meeting, we never kept in touch. It appeared that the Triolet family had recovered, they were doing very well. They appeared rather shocked that I was not. Today I wonder if those young people who were of my generation really understood our own village people's sacrifice when we accepted them in our lives at the start of the war. We suffered greatly trying to raise the funds needed to loge and feed them all. After the war they went home but received governments relocating and reconstruction benefits that we certainly never had.

Right after we had met, our contact was entirely lost, I was back in England shaping my departure for North America. The fault here is probably mine. I too, like Martin Luther King later said, "I had a dream". That dream took precedence over any unsatisfying relationship.

For me, back in Wellyn Garden City in Hertfordshire, working as a low wage domestic, I am still trying to accumulate those three hundred dollars in cash. I need to pay for my half of the government assisted ocean trip, it really appears to be an impossible achievement.

With my having to give this half part of a six hundred dollar sea passage all the way to Montreal, was an unbelievable huge troubled effort. I could not even spend much on PO stamps, so I was even avoiding writing to people. Remember that in my young years the post office was people's only connection.

My six months rather well paid cashier job at the American PX, had of course helped me a little but I still was not there yet. Before seeing a bit of light at the end of my tunnel, I had to wait six months working in England before being finally able to completely pay to Canada House those three hundred canadian dollars. Only then could I finally receive my trip ticket and that marvelous, authorized and legal work Visa.

Before I write on, I feel that I have to tell you why in my youth, our western part of France was so poor and a much depressed area for such a long period of time. The actual difficult period of the Great Depression had little to do with our poverty.

About one hundred and fifty years before that WW2 human tragedy happened and of course before the Ardennes refugees had arrived, our land had been a very good producing real estate. But why so poor since? What had happened a century and a half before to totally ruin our area?

At the end of the French Revolution, when the Republic was victorious and a new government was finally in place, a large part of the population of Vendee, had refused to abide by the new rules and caused many problems for the new regime.

Too many people had resisted and refused to take in the new concept. As punishment, Vendee was then attacked by a military action that almost totally destroyed, not just Vendee, but the entire Western France. My own ascendant people and their own homes and land, had been almost entirely wiped out of the map.

So who had committed such destruction? The armies were called Les Colonnes Infernalles, The Infernal Columns. Yes, and diabolical those armies certainly were.

It was done by some new Demonic French armies. They were created to kill and destroy very fast, an entire community, just like those of Hitler had done to the Jews and others supposedly not acceptable humans. The destruction was done with Hitler's newly and well-organized invented Schutzstaffel (SS) or like the Romans battalions had achieved in ancient history when they destroyed Hannibal's Carthage in North Africa.

So my home birth place, La Vendee of 1793, endured a total ruin and devastation! An entire farming population, all properties, all livestock, everything was massacred, killed, destroyed, burnt...The killing and destruction of everything in the punished Vendee was quickly achieved and although Napoleon Bonaparte called my ancestors The Giants and claim to honor them, at the time, he did nothing to stop the slaughter.

It finally ended when no more royalist leaders were to be found still alive to gather worried young boys to fight for a cause they did not understand nor agree with anyway.

Survivors at the time were my very own ancestors of the hills called the bocage. Some were hidden in caves. Since I am here to tell the story, it is obvious that some had survived. But over one hundred and fifty thousand people had been killed. It was what you can read today as the Vendean Genocide (Les Guerres De Vendee). I think the Vendeans did not have to pay taxes for something like fifty years after that there was nothing left, no farms, no animals, nothing.

France encouraged then the immigration to that poorest part of Vendee. This is why some daring young people from other unfortunate parts of the land took the gamble because of no taxes to pay for the fifty years and came to start their resettlement. They mixed with the survivors of the genocide and started new lives on the ruins of others.

I suspect that my paternal grandfather and his brother, having immigrated from another depressed part of central France had heard about those possibilities. They would have grabbed the chance to build a new life in our part of France.

I was asked once many years ago, how I would have felt if I had lived in 1793. It is always easy to speak out after the fact but in a way I feel that there was really no hope after that French Revolution. Why keep on refusing the new regime? The french king and his Austrian wife Marie Antoinette were already beheaded, what could be done then? They, and many of those aristocrats had abused enough of poor people anyway.

The smart ones, those Royalists who had been able to escape were gone abroad, many to America. When you hear of an old establish family french name in central USA now, it is very possible that their ancestors were the French Loyalists refugees of that time, lucky to have been received on this great American soil at the time of the French Terror.

After WW2, all our Ardennes Refugees who survived and went back home, did rebuild their homes and country. I am sure that Ardennes now is a beautiful part of France. The people I knew then in the war are possibly all gone for ever. If some should read this, please do believe that I think of you all, very often.

There is a funny situation I want to relate here about the Vendean punishment at the end of the French Revolution. My small part of France has always been sort of laughed at, considered as being a backward population. Well at least when I left this was the situation. Would you believe that most Vendeans still do not sing the French anthem La Marseillaise.

In 2015 when I last visited my dear old buddy Michel Leger in Poitiers, I reminded him how surprised I had been at age eighteen when I had seen his Dad chiseling off all the fleur de Lys from a lovely antique cabinet. Those decorations were the treasured emblem display of kings in France, and of all royalists in olden days. His reply was:" The wellbeing of my ancestors had been delayed because of those stubborn Vendeans, your ancestors who supported a beheaded king". He laughed. I believed that it was so strange to hear him say this after a 222 years. He told me his ancestors had blamed my Vendeans relatives as long as he could remember.

I laughed also, I am still laughing...OMG, how stubborn those old Frenchmen could be. Then suddenly my memory goes back to my twentieth birthday when I realized that Michel and I could only really be, just friends, nothing else. We were never encouraged by his parents. I guess the family of the distant Poitiers people wanted no alliance with those Vendeans after all. At the time, his father must have still believed that my ancestors, my family, all might be royalist and that, would never do.

I feel that for peace, I would be one who would most likely have accepted the new Republican ideas. Well now, let me think, my grandmother a descendant of those revolutionaries is still my idol, my star, the one who helped to raise me. She never would have given me a slap or pulled my hair of shoved me in anyway... I am going to drink my coffee right now, just the way she always did, not from a cup but from a bowl.

Life goes on.

In the Favelas

*I*n poor neighborhoods, I know by my own observations that the children do not have access to learning about all the activities I so wanted to do when I was a child. It is certain that many young ones should obtain help to learn about the arts, and the crafts and all those different things that usually fascinate children everywhere. Unfortunately, this is an extracurricular activity seldom found important to grownups when their survival is the primary concern.

As it turned out, when I was especially worried about Favelas children, I guessed I was right, so I went to check and worked with them for two years in South America. Why that part of the world? Because I had been strongly encouraged by two ladies I had met one day. I had told them about a certain plan I had formed in my mind and they assured me I could do well in their country.

From the very start, meaning from the first few days after I had arrived south, I wanted to show that the shoe shine boys might not have to be called by customers with a simple whistle or shout of "Lustra" or "lim-piabota". I showed the young boys who made a living for their families by doing this sort of job, that we could paint their first name on their workbox and I encouraged them to get their clients to notice it.

Above are some old pictures somebody had taken for me. One in particular shows one of the truckloads of merchandise sent to me at the end of the first year. Those were crates of good merchandise for the children with whom I worked and also for their families.

Hundreds of people who wanted to support my ideas had been involved. One preacher I had met in Texas, had told his congregation "Please my friends, I would like for you to send that lady the very best you have, no rubbish", just nice clothing. And, that is exactly what those darling good mortals had done, they sent me beautiful clothing.

With my having received such big aid, it allowed me to run a freelance program in a couple of favelas of South America with a certain simplicity. I made so many people happy with the donated gifts; This way I had better prospects of achievement while working with the children.

About my budget, before leaving the North, I had $300.00 of my own, my friend Josie Bullard from Houston had given me $300.00 and my friend Reg Heywood from Calgary who later became my fourth husband, had given me another $300.00. Reg had also given me a nice new stethoscope that I donated to a very poor young doctor I met while I hitch-hiked and stayed a few days in his village. He had never owned such medical instrument of his own, his work was strictly with the military camp of the village. His wife, also fed me and gave me water and soap to wash myself properly in their bathing shed.

Everywhere I stopped, I found children interested in painting, drawing, doing other crafts. Often the mothers would get involved. I recall one mother making lovely objects with the clay we were digging on the edge of a creek. After I left I guess she carried on teaching all the neighborhood children about that sculpturing she could do so beautifully. She said that she had never shown anybody about her talent. I remember the cute tiny pigs and other animals she would sculpture with clay.

I do not want to specify which country I had selected for my mission. Slums too often give a bad name to populations who strive at improving their lives and their social appearance. All south American countries are beautiful and so are their people. Many countries still have very poor neighborhoods that are overpopulated and are forever in need of upgrades. Their governments try all they can do to help, but it is not an easy job.

One day in the north, I had met a certain South American ambassador who was so impressed with my plan after I was refused by a regular help organization that the gentleman had written for me a great reference letter. He asked all South American boundary authorities to give me their full cooperation and to please, let me pass. He explained my plan in a few words and said I should be helped by every border patrols.

With this reference, I received all sorts of assistance. Border securities were just wonderful. Many agents would ask truck drivers whose papers they cleared, to please take me with them on their routes, and all would accept to help me and all for free of charge. For two years, the letter with the stamp of an embassy gave me an open door everywhere I went. What a gift that was!

On my arrival way down south, I had securely placed my budget, that small amount of money in a bank but it soon was used up by the many requests of help I received here and there by young families in need. They were all in need! So, in a few days, nothing was left of the cash and I just learnt to manage without. I did the best I could since I knew that many other humans did the same.

One day I was robbed of the only twenty dollar bill I had kept for emergencies. I was lucky to still have my passport. After that situation and when most of my brushes and paints had somehow disappeared, so had parts of the chess set someone had given me, I kept the precious letter "pass borders" with my passport in a small pouch that I kept safely on my chest.

Once arrived at my destination there in the South, local people soon were helping me and in exchange I would do something to help them. For about four months, the local branch of the YMCA gave me the equivalent of $10.00 a month to assist their teachers in one of their schools and a free bed in a small attic room safely hidden from the world.

Later, a restaurant owner gave me the use of a tool shed in his yard where there was a bunk and I could lock myself in. There was water close by so I could wash myself. I also often got some food for doing some of the yard work. And of course while moving about, I did what others did, I slept outside where ever I could find a spot fairly safe or hoping that it would be a rather risk-free place. Often it really was not. Once I woke up on a park bench where I had spent most of the night and on the next bench, a man had been murdered. With my being very tired, I had slept through the whole dramatic event.

When I had sort of settled my bones in one place after arriving at my final destination, some government officials having learnt of my project working with their poorest and very underprivileged children, realized I was doing everything alone. One of their agents came to speak with me and very quickly decided to give me his help. So when I was trying to clear custom for all my north-American gifted goods, another of the officials hired a truck and a few volunteers went to pick up from the harbor, the close to three truckloads of supplies I had just received. Those were the wonderful gifts that all my friends and many other people who wanted to help, had gathered for me in North America. See the picture of the last truckload.

At this point of my story I want to say that a young German family by the name of Roland and Connie Yelleh (or Jelleh) and their young children took me under their wing and made sure I would not starve. I also met Connie's visiting brother, a German doctor who sewed me up one night when I had an accident and needed help urgently. Two days before, somehow a bus had driven close to me and had hit a long piece of lumber that had been thrown flying into my legs and caused serious damage to my right tibia. I was in real trouble. Thank you again dear German family. Thank you to the Yelleh family medic who made sure my leg would be all right. Roland was an engineer hired for a huge water project.

I cannot possibly count how many wonderful North American people had helped me to gather all those goods for the favela children. Church groups, TV news people, friends of mine and so many strangers I would have loved to meet. Hundreds responded to my call for help. When these angels had learned of my project towards the end of my first year South, all had helped me in two short weeks, had accumulated close to 3 tons of clothing, a few art supplies, shoes etc...and one small TV set that the Y put to work right away when we unpacked the goods. I am talking of 1980, times have changed.

I had said that my people needed a lot of useful things and my disadvantaged multitude needed some items badly. People of the favelas had told me that they always needed clothing and when they saw what suddenly was arriving, they said that the "heavens had opened up and I had fallen from the sky, to land in their midst". What a divine and glorious praise.

A very generous North American gentleman by the name of Mr. Galbraith had paid to move all those crates at his own expense by train and ship. In my heart today, I still bless Mr. Galbraith and all those angels, those wonderful souls who trusted in my ideas.

So I stayed and worked with those Southern children for two years. Then I had to return home and make a living to survive the best I could. Life had to go on. I wanted to enjoy my own family and their descendants now.

Before I go on, I want to mention something newsworthy. While I was working in the slums one day a couple of old ladies, bare-feet and in rags, some ladies I knew well since they were living in those well known cardboard shacks, asked me if I had a couple of coins to give them. I never had anything to spare in the way of give away money but I asked those two grandmothers what was their project. They said the Red Cross needed cash and they had been asked to volunteer to gather a little bit of money, they had been asked to take a collection to help... The Poor... now, please, go figure that one out.

While on my mission, from age fifty to fifty two, I was going through menopause without even noticing it. When you help bury a child at least once a week, your hot flashes really do not matter very much. Typhus and other diseases played havoc among poor children in those days...1980 to 1982.

Somehow I had not worried enough about all my own vaccines and one day a group of Doctors without Borders got hold of me and made sure I was properly immunized. They had set up their clinic on the side of a road and were sort of checking on people walking by. I saw mothers not wanting to even listen to these doctors. They were just running away. Their children were dying but they did not trust those dedicated beloved doctors. Again, a lack of education.

While running my program as my own "show", I tried to help many little ones who did not go to school, I fervently hoped that they could learn something from me and, as you guessed it, in the end, I know they did but I learnt a lot from them also.

The children's families were always happy if I could do something for them too, such as hair cutting, lice search, foot massages, back massages, removing worms from feet, by pulling those out of their feet sores. People walking bare footed in rubbish too often get sores and the worms have to get out of those painful bubbles.

At this stage I should mention that in the crates, I had received lovely new shoes but the old people who had never worn shoes could not walk with the new footwear. One lady told me her entire life she had wished she would wear shoes but never had any. Now she tried so much but could not walk with them.

There were many tasks I could help the barrio people with and often I was given a bit of their food. I never asked but I was often hungry and they could tell. Poor people are often ready to share the little they have.

One day, I set a little six year old girl's broken arm. The child had been suffering for over two days without anybody doing anything to her badly broken arm. The next day when I came to check on her, the mother said she had to remove my makeshift cast because the girl kept crying in pain having had no pain killers. That's when I walked that child to the local hospital.

Once there, I begged for help and mentioned that I was fighting for The "Year Of the POOR Child", I hoped it was a project *finally* being discussed by the UN who had ignored me long before when I had tried to place the needs of poor children ahead of other causes.

I was a nobody and the UN never had wanted to listen to me. Later they listened to someone who probably was paid $150,000.00 a year working in one of their offices. Anyway, later on, yes the year of the child was decided and voted in but by then I had done my two years for the poor children and wanted to enjoy my own family. I had encouraged all along, many people to do the same if they could do it. Today I would not. Many parts of the world might be too unsafe places for my kind of missionary work.

So, back to the child with a broken arm; surprisingly, the medical staff of the local hospital where I took the girl, was very understanding. They said if the girl had been brought to them when the accident happened, they certainly would have looked after her free of charge.

Since I was not a relative of the little girl, I had to go find the mother in the barrio. I left my little patient with a nurse and I finally located the girl's mother. A woman in her mid twenties who had two other children and was trying her best anyway she could, to make money any way she could, for food every day. She followed me to the emergency and once there, she started a demonstration of crying and embracing the child as though she did not know the girl had had an accident. The medics said they were used to this sort of theater.

Women in the favelas had confided to me that most of them had no real legal husband but they would live with, meaning share a shanty, with a man who made them feel happy and who managed to get them some food. Why did they disclose this to me? Because when they realized that here were tons of clothing arriving from Northern families wanting to share their belongings with them, they had to confess something to me. They all had lied to me. Nobody was legally married, they would get babies and manage the best way they could to survive. So, everyone of them had given me a false name. It is often difficult to help the needy isn't it!

These women always figure that a child will grow up to be their deliverance. This strange plan idea does not always work. In fact it seldom does. Instead of a new baby being a liberating achievement for them, an added child often places more worries and responsibilities on their shoulders. And of course it is another mouth to feed.

I was horrified sometime when I saw for example, people's mouth having been chewed up by rats during the night when a baby sometimes left alone must have been screaming with pain and nobody had come to the rescue.

It appears that frequently, the ignorance of people living in those favelas is unbelievable. Most of those people especially the ladies never went to school so how would they learn anything beside trying to survive as slum mothers.

The South American medics always look after their people but if nobody reports an emergency, how can they treat it. Anyway that day I was happy to see that the child I brought to them was put to sleep, the arm was re-broken and reset and a cast was applied. It would be removed later on by a doctor at that same hospital.

Many readers do not know and cannot imagine the situation in which the poorest people of our world can manage to survive. Most of the time, the unfortunate and very underprivileged will not complain, some prefer to endure life in silence, thinking nobody cares. It is in reality, not the case. Unfortunately, too often, yes, their situation came from their own making, but really, who is to blame? This is an ageless, an eternal dilemma.

Most governments do care about their poorest citizens. However, the lack of education of such people as I already mentioned does too often cause them so much damage.

When a member of the federal government decided to find out what I was all about in that one particular favela, an official at the upper echelon, became my ally and allowed me to do my own thing, he told me a very interesting story right from the start of our semi friendly relationship.

On the edge of town, the municipal government, having been helped with a federal grant, had purchased several acres of good productive land, then donated to each family group, not cardboard, but enough planks of wood and corrugated roofing metal for all families to build themselves a good small house. Even volunteer builders were available to help and advise. Each family unit could even have a small garden patch. Just think what an improvement that could make in the lives of those very poor people. But the only important thing they wanted in their palm was hard cash. For so many people, there appeared to be no better power than dealing with the unmistakable medium of exchange.

Within a month all the material had been sold out to other people in town who took advantage of the cheap goods and the poor families were back in cardboard shacks among tons of garbage, in the center of town on the river's edge. No wonder people claim like Jesus did, that the poor will always be among us.

For the two years I was trying to teach the children what I knew. It may not have been very much to a university professor but to these children I could do magic with my arts and crafts instructions. At Christmas once we had made a giant nativity scene with a huge display of papier mache animals and people representing the three wise men. Visitors were coming to the slum to see the new show and take pictures. That made my young artists feel important.

So after my two years were over, I was actually done with my project, I started North. I did not wait to find out about how much prize money a certain YMCA received. A big Japanese arts show to which I had entered *all* the art work of my favela children, gave that Y, large money prizes. I had told the Japanese sponsors that if there should be prize money coming, to please give it to the Y. They did.

Just before I left, I was informed that *all* my favela artistes had won awards with their beautiful art work. I was very happy about this. The Y had taken the responsibility of mailing my huge parcel of art work to Japan.

It might help you now to see a map. When you arrive in the furthest northern part of the South American land, you end up on a narrow neck, a piece of land, a jungle called La Darien.

I do not know if finally now, today, a road has been built on that corridor connecting the South continent to the North landmass but there was a time when the jungle just kept taking back the land and roads could not be built across La Darien. Transport of humans and goods was always done by ships, on either Pacific or Atlantic ocean on each side of that land neck.

I walked a lot while going there, living in the South and going back home. I was helped by hundred of people who gave me rides. I hitch-hiked most of the time. Often, even a bus would stop and get me some distance for free.

Somehow traveling north to get myself back home any way I could, I had found my way to that one unsafe jungle spot where I had been advised earlier, not to go. I got off a fishing boat somewhere on the Atlantic side, walked many miles on forest trails trying to get to that neck of land and for some reason found my way walking up on a plateau, a place where several guys in charge there had a couple of small planes coming and going. It looked like there was a very serious "business enterprise" going on, so much activity.

After a surprised man wrote down my name and the number of my passport on a piece of paper, he gave me back my document. I was I happy about that! I wanted my passport to stay in my possession at all time.

Something I found out later was that I had somehow, while walking in the jungle, passed a border without knowing about it and was within Columbia without permission for my being now in this country.

Later on, I was helped very graciously to sort out my forbidden and very illegal entry by some very understanding agents on the other side of the border, on the Panama side. Let me say it again: Most people are wonderful.

But as I had entered the plateau where I saw the small planes, I was told that I should wait there, anywhere would be safe for me the "boss" had said, and he added there was no way I could find my way out on my own anyway. I would have to find a spot later on one of their small planes. I was told that my departure could take a little while.

That's when I started to walk back and forth on the forest edge of an open field along that landing plateau. Then suddenly, I disappeared in the jungle. I give you just one guess where I was.

So now, I kept on going, and further down a path, two, possibly three miles into the forest I met a surprised couple, a man and a woman who lived there in a cabin temporarily or full time, I did not ask them. All I recall is that they were rather friendly, tall people and rather skinny.

I suppose they were employed perhaps by the business company I had met...The man said that yes, he knew how to get me to the other side of the forest but what did I have to pay them. All I owned was a vombilla, a sort of tube pipe that filters your drink of the south american tea, mate (with acute accent on the e). The woman accepted it.

Now the man took me for a few miles all the way where I could hear the ocean, It had to be the Atlantic. There was no way I could be on the Pacific side since I had guessed that it would take over a week walking to the west side of the Darien. If you look at a map, it will help to understand where I was.

I would like to mention that when I was a very young child, my maternal grandmother was insisting that I should know what she called my *cardinal points*. As a five year old I already knew how to tell the North, South, East and West very well. Today don't ask me because I get sort of confused. In later years I tried to educate my children on this important matter. I wonder if they remember. Perhaps if one day they find themselves without their cell phone and without its GPS, they will have to remember those cardinal points.

So here I am now in the Darien jungle, La Selba the people had told me it was called. Night is going to fall very soon and my guide obviously wants to go back to his place. His instructions are that I have to keep walking ...he pointed North and then he said I should follow the beach to a village. Yes, you guessed it, I was just about to leave a very unsafe place.

The man said I had not paid enough with a vombilla, he wanted more, so yes I paid him what he wanted. To me at this stage, trust me, my survival and keeping going was better than self-respect, dignity or pride. I just wanted to stay friendly, cheerful, but at this point, I especially wanted to stay very much alive.

On my way North, later on, and after falling asleep on the beach, I woke up with a couple guys staring at me. I got a ride with them on their small motor boat and somehow got off after being sea sick but made it on land again. A few small fishing boats later, a very helpful crew dropped me on the SanBlas Peninsular and here now I was welcomed and stayed for a couple of weeks with families of Cuna (or Kuna) Indians. Yes, I certainly can say the word Indians because that is what, to me, they called themselves.

I must point out to you all before I forget it: a couple of Kuna fathers asked me one day if there was a way to bring a few North American Native boys to their peninsular because they so wanted to get some mixture in their group. I guess they are right, those people are getting maybe too mixed within their own people.

The Kuna people are a hard working bunch of citizens making a living fishing, growing and selling coconuts, bananas and plantains. A few young people spoke spanish. Their lives are free of unnecessary things and when I was there I did not see any junk food. The older ladies who by the way like all the Kuna women, young and old, do have a ring in their nose, tried to teach me how to paddle their home made hollowed out tree trunk canoes. I did not achieve the attempt very well, in fact I did not at all and had to be helped off the canoe...I had kept going in circle. That sure gave them all some good laughter anyway.

The village's name was Anachucuna, the tribe's name was Tule-Nega and the territory is actually part of Panama. I remember two little girls crying and running to their mothers, they had never seen a white face before.

I felt very much at home with these wonderful Indian people, I taught them to bake my french bread with a home made leavening starter, we made a temporary oven with earth and it worked very well. I also designed many new art works for their molas (blouses) and saburays (wrap-around square material they use as long skirts).

I befriended a neighbors family whose son was attending Moscow university, imaging, a Kuna student, in Russia. The family gave me an address in Anachucuna, to which I could send them later a dictionary, English and Spanish. I did, and am hoping that today one of their government officials has a good position. The gentleman probably speaks many languages including Russian.

A young Kuna man who had a recorder supposedly purchased in Panama City by his father, might still listen to all the songs of my repertoire. The day I left he played his music very loud and when I was rather faraway getting on a fishing boat that would take me further, I could hear my voice in the distance, singing all sorts of songs.

I had recorded for the young man just about every tune I knew, even a few songs in Spanish and the Kuna ladies taught me some in their own language. I am afraid to sing them for you now in case it contains some words that may not be acceptable. My Kuna friends were grinning a lot when I sang them. But never mind, here goes one song they taught me, supposedly a lullaby: the hhmm is a sort of humming...

Banni galaopoenai taey hhhmmm
Maha novie alli hhmm biyelly todaee
Ibiay vinapoee biyel y todahay
tunatolaviviallay..hhhmmm
maylay llayvoalle hhhmmm
Eli uwaso machido la vivigay hhhmmm
yamiga lawaso alley... there are many other verses.

I wrote several other lines of their humming song and am still keeping those hoping the people who sang it for me as I wrote it and repeated it, had a clean mind...but maybe they were only making fun of my accent.

The rattle they made me shake while singing it gave me a feeling that I might be made fun of, but maybe not. I loved those people and I was ready to believe and trust them. I just worried a little since I had been made fun of, and certainly fooled many times in my life, before.

With my Indian friends The Kunas, I ate green boiled bananas, but one day since I like the ripe ones, I stole a piece of ripe banana from their monkey, I also ate some of their own harvested wild rice. They called it mountain rice. I also had helped the women to pound the grain with a huge hand pestle in a hollowed tree trunk. The wild rice was now boiled with grated coconut and fish. Everything was wonderful, all was boiled and steamed, that is the sort of cooking I like the best anyway.

Thanks to UrbaGuaru a young girl who celebrated her ninth birthday one day, we ate smoked iguana after her hair cutting ceremony when all her relatives could snip a small cut, off her hair. Very lucky omen I was told.

Someone had brought a piece of sea turtle to cook also. The ladies were horrified that I had a taste of this delicacy. It is supposed to be eaten by men only. They predicted all sorts of health dangers that could happen to me, a woman, because of my having taken a bite of the raw turtle meat. Actually, to me, it tasted like beef. And BTW, I am still waiting for the bad effects of my having eaten a piece of that sea turtle.

I was, as always, very impressed by these newly met people who live a simple life in the wild, these dear Kuna people. I had bumped into many other southern tribes but had never stayed more than a day or two with them since at the time, my traveling was pushing me in either to the North or to the South.

While traveling, there had been only one group of very ancient mixed Indian people in whose village the truck taking me on the top of their banana load had driven very fast across that village. That day, the two men in charge of the said truckload were throwing stuff to the people running along the sides. They did not slow down nor stop.

Once we were miles away it was explained to me that in that particular village the truckers must never stop, just pay tole with gifts of goods and speed out of there. Too many people who stopped had disappeared. Our lives are in danger in that place they told me.

As soon as I had arrived, they wanted to keep me. In all those sort of old lost villages of South America, especially the women and the children wanted me to stay with them. I was someone new, something different in their lives. All promised I would be living well with them. I am sure they meant it.

I recall one old lady from another part of the further Southern world, pointing out to me one day that a spring was coming from the mountain and pouring the stream in several connected tree trunks down to where they lived. She made me understand that I would never run out of their clean water. What a glorious life giving gift now that I recall the offer.

When I arrived at the Kuna village of Anachucuna, I was told by a young boy that first I had to talk to the Elders. He wanted me to meet his Congresso. So I met his legislative assembly of several older men and was made right away to feel very welcomed.

The other gentlemen who had helped me off that very last fishing boat that was owned by some of their Kuna compadres, immediately built for me a sort of private toilet, a crouching spot in the sea.

Together they built for my private needs, a small fence and showed me how I would get privacy to do my natural body functions. Of course during that demonstration, all the ladies had a lot of fun but I was welcoming the offer and sure enough later on, used my own private toilet corner with many thanks to the guys who had built it.

I wonder how many of our so called civilized people might have given a thought to such an accommodation for the privacy of a visitor?

I was soon after, given my own hammock too and slept with about ten people of the same family. The Kuna ladies would walk around topless as soon as the sun went down. The molas or blouses they make, wear and sell are an artistic reminder of the body painting of the old past generations. I am adding here a few sketches I had made while I was with the Kuna people. I was offered to share an older lady's husband's in his hammock but I thanked her using the weary excuse. Culturally, this was very polite for the lady to offer the sharing of her man but I was not obligated to accept.

People's names I remember were: UrbaGuaru, Alicio, Cecilia...and many others I cannot pronounce. I will never forget my hospitable Kuna friends.

a lady Cuna taking her fruit to the purchasing boat

Anachücüna

Where do the Cunas live?

the red dot shows where Anachüciina is located. The black dots indicate some of the over 40 inhabited islands that are occupied by the Cunas.

green indicate jungle

Atlantic ocean

Panama

Pacific Ocean

Panama City

Colombia

dangerous wild area

If I had not had a family in North America, I feel that I might have settled nicely in some of those villages of South America. I might have lived there for a year or longer, maybe a few years even, who knows. Everywhere I stopped, I felt so welcomed by everybody.

After leaving the village of Anachucuna, I found my way to Colon at the end of the Panama famous Watercourse and followed the canal all the way to Panama City. There I found the Canadian consulate.

The diplomat was a nice lady who, to my surprise, said:

"I am glad you are alive, two weeks ago, I received a radio message from someone in Colombia; It said that a lady with a Canadian passport had ended up at a spot of La Darien, then had disappeared in the jungle. Your name was given but when I reported you missing in our Ottawa office, I asked not to report this to your family yet...you do realize that you might have visited a very dangerous place don't you?" I had to agree with the lady. Then she added. Another place that I believe you might have crossed is the village of.......... where the people have kept many of their ancient beliefs. Truckers never stop there since several who did, never came out.

If now I look at the picture of a shrunken head, it makes me tremble and I think about a certain village way south of here.

All I knew is that I was alive and I was on my way home. Yes I find that all the people of the world are wonderful and fascinating. I am thankful to the "boss" at the tiny airport who did notify my consulate in Panama City about my having *disappeared* in the jungle. I thank him for caring.

My commitment of two years working with poor children being fulfilled, I now could start cleaning houses, then get married again, why not, I had done that a few times already right? And here now is a new chapter of my life, I call it ...not 91, but: 92 Years of love, Witnessing Of An Old Lady. The SEQUEL

Before going on with these olden days story details, perhaps I should mention why I had gone to spend two years of my life with underprivileged children. That wanting to help in the advancement of young ones has always been close to my heart.

As a 19 year old girl, I felt that I had lived a very miserable youth but I had survived WW2, when really so many people had not. In fact over fifty five million people had died in those long unhappy five years. After such bad historic period, I had found myself on the road to a better life after all, while waiting for my twenty-first birthday's emancipation. Than forever after and up till now, today.

Being not evidently extremely religious but never having discarded my secret correspondence with the God I was sure, had protected me, I had made a few promises to my heavenly forces while praying in a church of Poitiers.

My mother's handicap fixing was my first request of a cure. In 1946, Mom had gone through her one and only hip surgery, she did not walk much better than before since the system of the time was to cement the bones together preventing the femur from going further up in th ehip. After the surgery she could never sit down but only lien on a stool sideways, however her greatest pains now were eliminated and I had this out of my worries.

If you read my first book of Memoirs, you might remember that in my late teens, my then young friend Michel Leger would wait for me on Sunday morning outside that Poitiers church. After mass he would take me for a good meal and a great afternoon to his parents country house. In the big city the family had their retail business and their main residence.

But another very important promise I had made to Heaven was that one day in the future, I would donate two years of my life helping and working for the advancement of poor children.

Remembering how by chance one day I had befriended two ladies who shared those ideas of *payback* and they had suggested to me that in their certain birth country of South America, I could be very useful. That was how I was encouraged to just go there and carry on my mission. So, I would eventually do it...And so now, *I had done it.*

Finding my way home from the South American continent, here I am now going back to Canada to see my grand children. My first daughter Mary and her husband who live in Ottawa are expecting their first child, they will make me grandma to three adorable descendants who in time make me a great grandma numerous times. So will my other daughters.

When thinking back on the years, I do not think in my life I was ever bored. Perhaps a few times, as a child when it was raining heavily and I was house bound too much.

A friend of mine was asking me the other day:"Geny, you are 91 years old, you moved over fifty times, you married five times, you went around the world in more than eighty days, you wrote books, you spent two years with the poor children, you are still working and earning a living. You also still call yourself a street teacher, When will you stop?" my reply was:"When Jesus whispers in my ear: *it's time to go*".

Home again, 1982

My mission with the poor children is over now, my own life must resume, I must find work. I passed my 52d birthday, I stay a few weeks with my good friend Bernie and her family in Prescott, South Ottawa. Dear Bernie and her extended family have helped me so many times in the past. They do it again, I live with them, they get me jobs working with all their friends and relatives. But I do not want to impose so I place my work wanted ad on the bulletin board of the local Post Office.

That is how I meet a very gentle man called Hubert.

And here is where I want to pass the baton to his wife Debbie because this sweetheart of a young lady has a life story to tell and I would like for her to describe it to you my dear readers, my friends...

As soon as I met Debbie she finds me customers and plenty of work. For years I received a Christmas parcel from her and her Mom. She is still today one of the dearest mortals in my heart. One of the most interesting person I ever met. Here is Debbie's story:

The year was 1952, April 10th, no one living remembers the time, but a little baby girl was born in the Mattawa General Hospital. Deborah Elizabeth Baker (DEB) for short, was the second of eight children born to Rita Helen Gauthier and Keith James Baker. In chronological order of birth, the children were Eric, Deb, Leif, Velda, Glenda, Curt, Wade and Dale.

The Doctor who delivered me was Saint-Firmin Monestime, famous for being a Haitian-Canadian politician, and the first Black Canadian elected mayor of a Canadian municipality[1]. Seventy years later I still remember his large comforting hands and deep voice that from a child's perspective made him seem like a giant, but that created a deep-seated feeling of safety in me; something that I was utterly unfamiliar with at the time.

I only knew one Great Grandparent and that was my father's grandmother Risser. She came from Germany as a war bride and married my grandfather After several years and 3 children, my great grandfather left for work fishing in the Atlantic Ocean and his boat must have capsized because he was never heard from again.

My great grandmother Risser was musically talented and played he organ and piano. She was very good and sometimes musicians would visit her just to play along. Hank Snow recorded one song with her. She also published a book of poetry, only 100 copies made, but sadly no relatives have a copy and it has been lost to time. She owned what is now know as Rissers Beach Provincial Park in Petite Rivière along the South Shore Region of Nova Scotia. This property was left to my father when she died at 97, around 1964. [2]

---

[1] Mattawa is situated on the banks of the Ottawa and Mattawa Rivers along the foothills of the "Laurentians. " In the seventeenth and early part of the eighteenth century, two important Indian bands of the Algonquin Tribes, occupied this area. When the first white settlers arrived, the Mattawa River was the dividing line between the hunting grounds. The band leaders were Chief Antoine Kikiwiwies and Chief Amable Dufond. Chief Antoine's band hunted north of the Mattawa River including Rosemount, and Temiskaming area whereas Chief Amable Dufond's band hunted on the present site of Eau Claire, Rutherglen, and Lake Talon. The Chiefs named the area Mattawa meaning "The meeting of the waters." Over one hundred years later the Mattawa General Hospital occupies a site on Rosemount overlooking the two rivers.

[2] When the English had control of Nova Scotia in the mid-eighteenth century, they brought in many Palatine Germans to settle the area around today's Lunenburg. Some of these people and their descendants along with some English spread out to settle in adjacent areas such as Petite Riviere. The river provided access to the Atlantic Ocean. This access encouraged fishing and boat-building. By the nineteenth century tourists began flocking to Petite to enjoy its beaches and scenery.

The first picture is Risser's provincial park. The second pic is Great Grandma Risser and the third pick is Ezekiel Baker when he was in the army. (He is the one dressed in white)

My fathers parents were Meta-Ann and Ezekiel Baker. Back in the early 1900's they didn't have much. Grandpa was an ambitious man and he bought a property in Fall River, N.S. with what he was able to save when he worked on the docks at Halifax Harbour. He built a house and dug his own well. Grandpa even had a few amateur fights when he was young. He was previously married and had 5 children. When his wife passed away he married my Grandmother and raised 5 kids plus 3 more they had together.

Grandma and Grandpa were equal partners in everything except drinking alcohol (which Grandma thought was the devil in him). Grandpa worked on the docks, unloading ships and other odd jobs and he was part of the Shipfarers Union so was guaranteed so many hours a week. He built the house and everything else that he needed, by himself, while Grandma made everything from clothes to laundry soap. She planted fruit and vegetables and stored everything for the winter; there was no waste. Because they were better off than most they were also very charitable. Once a month (in a cauldron setup in the backyard) they would make a big stew, or roast, or soup with fresh baked bread, and would setup tables outside where all the neighborhood children could come over for a nice, hot meal. During the depression there was a lot of starvation and my dad used to say that for a lot of those children it was the only hot meal they had in a week.

Because they lived through the depression era, everything was used, reused, saved and cherished both out of habit and out of fear that another depression might arrive. Once, when I visited my grandmother as a child, she served me breakfast; cereal with a bun on the side. This bun was as hard as rock so I didn't eat it, and just left it there beside my bowl. For lunch that same bun was beside my plate again, and I still refused to eat it. When supper finally came, there was that damn bun again. This final time I put it in my pocket when she wasn't looking, and later took it outside and used a rock to crush it to feed to the birds. So maybe it wasn't put to the use she had intended, but it certainly wasn't wasted.

Grandmother served tea with our meals and tea was hard to get during the depression. After we would have our tea, she would hang the tea bag on the clothes-line and let it dry to use a second time. After the second time, she would put it in a bottle with all her eggs shells and fill it with water to feed her plants.

Grandpa died at around the age of 60 leaving Grandma to raise all eight children on her own. Grandma sold gravel from her land to buy a cow (for milk) and she basically made everything else. Whenever she needed money badly she would sell another load of gravel, so with all her hard labour they survived. Grandma died at 87 (1903 – 1990).

To this day, I still remember my brothers and sisters, parents and grandmother going to the launching of Bluenose II in 1963 in Lunenburg, Nova Scotia which can still be visited today. The champagne bottle missed the boat on the first try, which eleven year old me found hilarious.

My mothers parents were Susanna Bertha St. Denis 1904 – 1987 and Leonard Gauthier 1904 – 1936. Again, my grandfather build the house they lived in, in Mattawa. He was also ambitious and worked on the railway and odd jobs to help support the family. My grandmother did everything in the home, made clothes, grew food, preserved for the winter. She had several bins in the basement with potatoes, carrot and other assorted vegetables, along with a coal shute that the truck used to pour the coal down for the winter. This was the time when all clothes washing was done by hand and the making of dresses, pants, shirts, socks, underwear etc was done with needle and thread. Everything was time consuming and scheduled, bread making one day, laundry one day and usually everyone had a bath on Saturday so you were ready for church on Sunday. And, everyone shared the same bath water because you had to heat the water in a kettle for the bath, and you just added another kettle full for each couple of kids.

In 1936 penicillin and other antibiotics were not easily accessible and after a 10-day battle with pneumonia, my grandfather passed away at age 33 leaving my grandmother to raise five children on her own. Sadly, pneumonia continued to plague my family. My baby brother Wade passed away from pneumonia at age 44, and we almost lost my sister Velda to it as well, though she eventually made a full recovery.

There were no death or child benefits back then and after my grandfather passed, my grandmother worked long hours on other peoples laundry and cleaning while she did the cooking, mending and raising of five kids. Several years later she remarried and had a sixth child, Garth.

My grandmother Susanna was the brightest, fairest, strictest, woman that I have known and I loved her dearly. She was a wonderful woman, with a fantastic sense of humor who always thought about others before herself. She could add numbers up faster than you could read them, she was great at cards and improvisation. She did not drink but I still remember a time when we sat out on her step and shared a beer and a cigarette and reminisced about the past. She was my role model.

This Is my grandmother Susanna

My parents, Rita Helen Gauthier 1926–2015 and Keith James Baker 1926 – 2020 met in Nova Scotia while selling Maclean's magazines. When they met, my mother had a child from a previous relationship with a man who passed away. She had given this child up for adoption because, at the time, my mother was alone and working but could not support the child and wanted a better life for him. Later my mother and father looked for the child, but at that time you did not have to reveal the adopted parents, so they never found him.

They lived in Nova Scotia for about two years, and my older brother Eric was born there. My parents then moved to Mattawa temporarily while I was born, spent a brief time in Ottawa, then finally settled in Lindsay, Ontario. We first lived in a small apartment above a store with very little heat and no way to wash clothes except in the bathroom tub. After a few years renting, my parents bought an older home that still had the special green paint you used to get during World War II and tartan wallpaper on the ceiling in the kitchen (which remails there today).

The older home had an outhouse and no running water. Over the years my father put a full bathroom in, changed the heating from one wood furnace in the living room to a full basement oil furnace and renovated the rest of the house, putting in plumbing and wiring, and all other conveniences. Basically gutted it and started over. I remember many (up to 10 coatings of wall papers on the walls and behind it places where all kinds of flies and bugs got in. He built storm windows and sheds and basically refinished the 75 year old home.

My mother was resourceful, raised 8 kids, made clothes, knitted, crocheted, made afghans, blankets, mitts, scarves, all while working full-time. Mom worked at the Britain Carpet Factory fixing and making carpets for all kinds of companies. The building she worked in had no air conditioning and sometimes it reached temperature of 101 degrees. Back then workplace safety per-cautions were not the same as they are today and the carpet particles in the air were unfiltered by ventilation or face masks. My mother had breathing problems throughout her life and spots on her lung that we suspect can be attributed to her work at Britain Carpet. My mother continued to work into her senior years, both at the Lindsay Pool and at McDonalds.

Times were hard and money short growing up in Lindsay, and although we always had enough to eat, there was very little else. My father found it difficult to find stable work that paid well. He first delivered bread, then worked in a furniture store, then worked at the Lindsay Brakeshoe factory, and was eventually self-employed doing seamless flooring for which there simply wasn't enough demand. As an older individual (around 50) he went back to school and took his grade 12 equivalent and welding and other courses and graduated with diplomas in all. Dad was a pilot as well and at one point owned his own plane.

My father was always an angry man, unhappy with certain aspects of his life. He was very intelligent but lacked the education needed to pursue a career in any kind of scientific or academic field. In addition to this, he only ever wanted one child, but my mother, as a Catholic, could not access birth control. Adding fuel to the fire, when he was young he drank a lot, and although the drinking stopped as he got older, the anger never really left him. There were many times when we kids went to school with bruises all over our bodies. Influenced by this treatment, all eight children left home by age 18, most by age 16, and some have struggled with substance abuse and mental illness, as well as anger issues and physical abuse as adults. The impacts of childhood trauma can be long lasting and show themselves in different ways.

Dad was also an intelligent man that could build anything out of steel or wood. While in Halifax he worked as a Seamans cook and this is one of the comments he sent me in an email "THERE'S A HURRICANE HITTING FLORIDA WITH 130MPH WINDS; I EXPERIENCED ONE JUST LIKE IT BACK IN THE EARLY 40s. WE WERE OFF CAPE HATTEROUS WHEN IT HIT US, WE WERE DOING 15 KNOTS, HEADING NORTH; A DAY LATER WE WERE MAINTAINING THE SAME SPEED AND WERE 45 MILES 'SOUTH' OF THE CAPE. WE HAD WAVES 45' HIGH. THE WEATHER REPORTS NOW PREVENT THAT FROM HAPPENING. ONE GUY HAD A HARD TIME OF IT BUT HE WAS JUST NEW. IT DIDN'T BOTHER ME; I WAS JUST GRATEFUL THAT IT HAPPENED ON OUR WAY BACK; {WE HAD JUST DELIVERED 2000 TONS OF GYPSUM, (ROCKS) TO JACKSONVILLE FLA. ....THE FIRST WAVE WOULD HAVE PUT US IN DAVY JONES LOCKER.} THE US AIRCRAFT CARRIER," ENTERPRISE", WAS HEADING FOR IT'S HOME BASE IN NORFOLK VIR., AND THEY MEASURED THE WAVES.(OUR RADIO MAN TALKED TO THEIRS.). I WAS NEVER SEASICK"

If you visit the museum in Mattawa you will see my mother's picture as one of the first grade 10 graduates. She is in the flower print in the middle of the first row. The last pic of Dad and Eric as a baby

~~~~~~~~

I was born in 1952 and was raised and naturally inclined to care a lot for others. I was taught that girls were meant to get married and have babies and not worry about education or the future. I had very little self-esteem. We all started working at a young age first delivered newspapers then babysitting to help bring in money. Unfortunately, some of the people we delivered to were nasty; NEVER allow children to go into a strangers homes alone. I started babysitting at age 12 until the day I turned 16 and was allowed to work in a clothing store. In my spare time I helped mom with chores, taking care of my siblings, and buying clothes for the family. It was understood that all of the money I made would go back into the household to help feed and clothe the children. At one point I was going to school and working 40 hours a week besides, which obviously had a negative impact on my grades and limited my access to any future education. My mother didn't have her last child until I was 18.

Without access to any other options and desperately seeking freedom, at age 19 I met and married a guy after dating for a year. My husband Hubert and I lived in Inkerman Station, the home of the first paid hockey team (the Inkerman Rockets) Six months after I was married I knew I had made a terrible mistake, not only did my husband cheat on me, but this was the beginning of his verbal abuse. At the time, there was no way out; my parents believed you stayed and fought your battles but you never left your husband. I was raised to be subservient in every way and was so naïve, I couldn't imagine doing anything else besides being the best wife and mother I could be. The marriage went on for 9.5 years, the best parts of which were the births of my two children; my beautiful daughter Michelle Marie in 1974, and my fantastic son Aaron Jonathan in 1976. Over time, the marriage turned violent and I finally packed it in with the kids and moved to the projects in Ottawa

During this time my ex got a housekeeper and on one of my visits I had the privilege of meeting Geny Heywood. She had just arrived from South America and was cleaning and painting houses, and babysitting. Right away I liked her and had great respect for all she went through. Throughout the following years I would find work for Geny where I could. She babysat for me for a while, but it was hard because we were poor.

We started over, in Ottawa, in 1980 when I was 30. I didn't have a full time job, worked at Revenue Canada for 4 months a year. I had to collect unemployment for the first winter to pay the rent and I was very embarrassed about that. We didn't really have a xmas that year, I tried to knit a scarf and mitts for the kids. Michelle made me a beautiful turtle pin cushion out of rags and Aaron made me a colouring book picture with a red paper frame. These gifts I still have and were the most wonderful things. In the spring I was able to find a permanent job as a clerk at a granting council. This was very good work and I learned a lot about computers (up to that point I hated the way they consumed everyone's time). I stayed there for three years then moved on to contract work with the federal government.

We were poor but I told myself that we would do better. I would rent out a room to make extra money for clothes and things for the kids. I did this for many years to pay the bills, education, food, clothing, dentist and any other essential thing that was needed.

In 1990 during an abusive relationship, and suffering from undiagnosed bipolarism, my ex committed suicide. It was a shock to us all and was very hard on my children. I'm sure many people have experienced this and can attest to the long-term trauma it can cause.

I met a wonderful man and we saw each other occasionally, when time permitting, over the period of 20 years. I was full of hate and anger and with his help I was able to resolve most of my issues. That was until shit started happening again.

Throughout these years I did a lot of charity work. Volunteered as district coordinator for the Kidney Foundation, canvassed for the Heart Institute; was the treasurer on an Environmental committee and coached baseball and softball.

In 2006 one of my brothers passed away from pneumonia, unexpectedly. Soon after I lost my mother and father-in-law, then another brother had a massive heart attack and died but they were able to resuscitate him. A sister went in the hospital with pneumonia and while they were testing her they punctured her lung and she almost died. And then yet another brother had a terrible car accident and almost died. I then lost my wonderful man and just when I thought I couldn't take any more, Revenue Canada decided to audit self-employed contractors and charge them for claiming expenses. This process with Revenue Canada lasted 3 years, and I had to sell my home to pay the lawyer, accountant and them. I had the best tax layer in Ottawa and Revenue Canada refused to meet with him. We formed a lobbyist group that made Revenue Canada seize and desist but, unfortunately the people that they had charged, illegally, were made to pay. The ruling proceeded to go into force the following year.

So there I was at 57, starting over again. I rented a friends condo and while working I spent the next 10 years helping my senior parents, mom had moved to an Ottawa seniors residence and dad remained at home about 4 hours away. Back and forth we would go once a month. Mom liked to make dish clothes and dish towels and every Christmas Geny would receive a new one.

Later another brother passed away from cancer. Another dreaded disease that I'm sure most people can relate to.

Through the years I had the privilege of attending many music concerts and festivals and these were part of the highlights of my life. Two of my brothers and two sister have also had concerts. Music is the best remedy for the soul. I've met a lot of people over the years and many of them are friends to this day. Some people are wonderful.

My daughter found a dog for sale that I could buy for my son in 2007 Christmas. His name is Vision and he has helped me through a lot of hard times. He lets me screw with his head and plays practical jokes on me. His love is unconditional, my love for him the same and every day he is here I am thankful.

My children are very talented. My daughter has written a movie and several plays and had sculptured some of the best three dimensional characters I've ever seen. My son works on Warhammer models, cleans, paints and builds armies.

And now, as I approach the winter side of life I feel content. I could have done more but it's not over yet. I would wish to undo the hardships my children have faced and given them more happiness but the future is open.

In closing, I wish to say one last thing, my friend Geny is the most remarkable person I have had the privilege of knowing and I want to thank her for allowing me to share my memories and life with you.

Here I am Geny, back talking to readers. I am sure you find Debbie's story fascinating. I sure do. Thank you Debbie for allowing us to learn from your life such valuable information about so many historic years. I always love to hear my friends telling me about their past. Several were invited to share but so far Debbie is the one who was daring enough. Thank you dear Friend of…thirty nine years!

So now in 1982, as soon as I am back home after my two years in South America, I find everybody still so wonderful, I get help, I get work, I have my own income and have many friends. Now I buy an old abandoned log cabin in need of huge repairs and start fixing it.

My dear Reg Heywood comes all the way in his truck from Calgary to help me. He brings all his tools and his credit card. In no time he has to go back to look after his own house but by then my cabin is livable and my friend Adrienne wants it.

My friend Adrienne Sauve is a year younger than I am, she had been a Catholic nun, a teacher then a government counselor for most of her life. She buys my new property but what she wants is the beautiful location of my cabin, the place, the land. She buys it for the realty then on it, builds a two bedroom bungalow with all the updates that she said she could not live without. She donates the log cabin to the Boy Scouts, they dismantle it and move it somewhere else.

In no time at all, Reg and I finally get married, remember we were engaged for three years by then. We set housekeeping on an acreage close to the Saint Lawrence River where we stay for many years as pioneers wannabee till his death at age 88. I gave many details about life before, with Reg, and after Reg. I hope you read the first book.

For me now, today, entering 2022 going on 92 years of age, it is time to think about preparing myself to slowly getting to the conclusion of life. I am already living very close to my grown up children whose young healthy families are expanding. Even my grand children are leaving home and are going to fly on their own. They are now building their own future.

Where did it all fly away so soon? Most of my children have retired. A short time ago they were babies, my babies. If you are missing details in my Memoirs. If interested you might like to read "91 Years Of Love, Witnessings of An Old Lady" if you have missed that story. That first edition is raising funds for Veterans Charities.

Here now, I am adding a few episodes I think are important to my narrative. I thank you for having read the story so far. Please accept the blessing of this old woman. As the Scottish people would say "May your chimney smoke for many years".

People in My Prayers

*W*hen I start thinking about all the people I have loved over my many years on this earth, I feel like making a list just to prove to myself that indeed I have not forgotten them. I still remember these dear good-natured people so often. They were, and they still are since many younger ones are still around, not my family members, they were and they are, people towards whom I felt and still feel a truly heartfelt tenderness. To me the word Love has never meant sexual activity, it is a heart thing.

Yes, I can truly say that word, *love*. You know and understand how that word defines a very special warm feeling that you hold in your soul for certain people but not necessarily for others you probably also like very much but not truly love.

The very first person I recall with tender feeling was...**Madame Cornuault**, a neighbor I admired very much. I was probably not even two years old when I first met her. I will never forget her because of her being always so amiable to me when I was a child. You could tell she adored children, her own three, Jeanne , Andre and Henri, but also all the other children around the neighborhood. She just loved all children.

Last time I was in my village I met her son Andre, a man a year older than I am. I told him how much I loved his Mom, I am sure he knew that I was not the only person in the world who honored his mom's memory.

When the war started, a certain Parisian actress had worried about her only child, a seven year old daughter. The young mother had inquired from an old lady she had met who used to live in our village but had moved to the capital to be with her own grown up children. Would the senior lady by any chance know of someone who could keep a child safely in their home? Right away Madame Cornuault's name had come up and the child spent four years safely protected, under this lady's wing.

I remember meeting the young girl at the bakery in 1939, the sales lady asking the new girl many questions. I remember so well when she asked: "How long will you live at Mrs Cornuault's home? The little girl had said: "Until the end of the war" This had made such an impression on me that I can still see that lovely little child sent to get her host family's bread and saying that she would be here living with that lady's family for the duration of the war.

Now about **Madame Bourget**, another lady who lived across the street from us when I was born. I recall that she would hold me in her arms, cuddle me, rock me back and forth, possibly because she had two boys, wonderful kids but she might have missed having a little girl.

When at age fourteen I was in boarding school in Fontenay, the city where Madame Bourget and her family had moved, one day I got my permission to go out for a visit and I surprised her. Madame Bourget made us a cup of coffee, well the chicory drink we all drank during the war and even long after. We each ate a piece of toast with her home-made jam. She was the first person in the world to show me that I could dunk my toasted bread with jam on it, in my chicory. It was all right, nobody would slap me. I dunked, I still do it, I loved it and have never stopped doing that dunking business.

Denise Poupin, the young lady I already spoke of in my first story about her Dad, the town crier. I also mentioned her parents being the janitors at city hall etc.. when I was very young Denise had advised me to read everything that would fall under my hands and I always did. She was born about two years before I was.

The poor young birth mother had died suddenly a few hours after Denise was born. Much later in years to come, I learnt from my mother that her dad, the town crier, finding himself suddenly widowed and with a baby, had gone a few streets around with his drum and said: "Avis...I am begging the help from a single lady to assist me. I have a baby girl who needs the love of a mother...". And after a quick other drum roll he had gone home crying.

The early next morning, one rather stern spinster came to him and said: "I shall raise your child as if she were my very own daughter". He married the lady a short time later when he found her to be true to her word, the lady never faulted.

Denise loved that lady dearly and I am not sure she ever knew that the lady she cherished and called Maman was not her real birth mother. I had learnt of that quick marriage-adoption story many years later from my own mother. I say it again, secrets were well kept in those days of my youth in our Vendee.

Mademoiselle Guillonet was a true academic who had been recalled to work at the start of the war since there were not enough teachers left men being gone to war, then in German camps and prisons. Practically all the men had gone to the front in 1939.

When I met that lady, right after the war, on my first day at the Luçon boarding school, she told me "do you know that many years ago I was teaching your father's sisters, Your now middle aged aunts?"

That should tell us that this lady was one rather senior teacher brought out of retirement when war started. She had to be good. She was a great instructor and I am really not surprised that she had been recalled. Not only did she have the patience of an angel, she knew how to explain all sorts of problems so we would understand them. She would open a door in our brains and oh what a feeling, to be able to really interpret a difficult lesson and to be able to really learn something new!

In my long life, I met very few people who actually knew how to really explain a lesson. I remember her telling us how one day in the future, people would be taking some sort of pills or candies to replace some missed nutrients. Every time I swallow a few vitamins, I think of Mademoiselle Guillonet who lived in a plain house built on beaten-up earth, no wooden floors. Mademoiselle Guillonet wore the clothing her mother had left her. Whatever money she had made teaching when she was young, had gone to help her two orphaned nephews who were in university.

Lizette Drapeau, a wonderful young lady, a teacher, who wanted us younger girls to learn and remember how to dance for the day when *the war would end* she said. She would promise to us that one day would come and we would be free and we would sing and dance. She wanted us to learn to dance. I have tears in my eyes right now thinking about Lizette.

She and I had become friends earlier because she had met, sort of fallen for, at a country fair, a boy who happened to be from my village. I had told her that I knew he was just about to get married any day now to another girl. Lizette understood and stopped dreaming about the young man of my village. His name was Lili Blanc.

Madame Allory. She was the principal at my girls' school. She tried to force my father into letting me finish my schooling. She wanted me to become a teacher. She did inspire me to never give up and learn something new every day.

Philippe Ganguza. A GI I knew and I liked very much, he was from New York city. No romance, just a good friend. He was found of a young lady I knew, but she died. He asked me in a letter to go to her grave to place flowers for him but I never could do it since I had left her area and was already in England when she was killed in a car accident.

After 55 years I found his tel number while searching the internet. I called and when I said: "Mr Ganguza , you would not remember me but..." suddenly he said: " of course I remember you Genevieve

Engerbeau". He said my name right away. I found out that he died before I received the long letter that he promised to send me that day on the phone. We had never even kissed. He was supportive of my artistic trials. Often in the evening, he and I would chat at the window of my rented room in La Rochelle.

Merry Melek was a former Miss Edmonton, a beautiful Ukrainian young girl, the grand daughter of my landlady, Mrs Shalts. Merry heard me say some words that I had learnt at work in a restaurant kitchen and she said: "Geny, let me tell you about words that are NOT OK to use in English..." I was grateful to this little woman who realized how vulnerable immigrants are when learning or using the language in a new country.

Last time I saw Merry Melek, was when she paid me to make her a dress. I sure welcomed that bit of cash. I was then expecting my second child. She was about to marry her sweetheart. She moved away. Later on, I too moved away.

Debbie Jackson is the age of my second daughter, born in 1957. she still lives in Ottawa Canada. 'Just retired recently because of her bad back. We met forty years ago while promoting the making of crafts for all children. I hear from this Deborah often by emails. We are both free-spirited women. Because of this attribute, her family really did not accept nor appreciate her extraordinary and often very contrary ideas. I am so glad that my own family takes me as I am. My children have never tried to change me...I am happy about that. They probably would never have succeeded anyway.

At one time, we, Deborah Jackson and I, did the flea markets together. She still calls me her surrogate mother and for many years when I lived in the far North, my telephone number was always in her purse as an emergency call.

Debbie Saint Pierre. This other Dear Debbie helped me by finding me all sorts of work when I returned from South America. I ended up being the cleaning lady for much of her neighborhood homes. Debbie and her Mom would send me parcels at Christmas time. I still have a small bottle of Avon's Skin So Soft that she had send me years ago in a huge box of goodies. She never minded that I loved her husband Hubert. I had met him before I met his wife Debbie. Hubert was another great buddy of mine, never my lover. I also knew he loved his wife but he had been very hard on her, had cheated and been abusive. Debbie had left him one day and taken her children. Hubert told me many times how much he regretted his trespasses but it was too late. He finally killed himself one day.

Bernie Mears and I met I think it is now over fifty eight years ago. I would be a regular guest with her large family at many of their Sunday dinners. My dear Bernie left us last year and I silently pray for her magnificent soul. When she had learnt that I was leaving for my South American slum odyssey, she made me a small package of things I would never have thought of taking with me. For example an astronaut sheet, silver on one side, gold on the other. Looks like foil but is a very soft and pliable protective sheet. She added a few dried pieces of meat, a tiny flashlight, a small package of Kleenex and a book of matches. Then in an empty can of tuna that she had washed and scrubbed well, she had rolled corrugated cardboard and poured melted candle on it. " light it when you are cold" she had said...I used every item from that tiny pack and found everything so helpful.

I used that tuna can with waxed cardboard when I was crossing central America and was surprised in a storm one night. I went to the next jail-house and asked to be placed safely away for the night. The policemen did! They watched me light a corrugated cardboard in a tuna can and marveled at how warm the tiny jail cell was in a few minutes.

Sylvana Louras is a first rate Niagara Falls real estate lady who truly knows how to help people in search of a home. Only Sylvana could have found for me over the years, the old houses I was looking for but that nobody else wanted to buy. Only she and I would see the potentiality of my purchase. She would always help me make them livable and brought me much of the furniture to complete my investments.

Living rent free has always been my design and with my low wage jobs Sylvana found me the possibilities to have no rent to pay and live paying just my taxes and insurances. I must also add that Sylvana fed me a great many times, gave me free theater tickets. I can imagine how her grand children love that dear lady, my very dear friend Sylvana.

Gary Armstrong My beloved Gary A, is an Irish born immigrant, an engineer I consider my very own walking encyclopedia. I can ask him anything, he has the right answer. Nobody else I know really could ever come close to the knowledge that such a man clutches in his brain. He loves people, loves the world he lives in. Perhaps because he is a Freemason, I do no know for certain but to me those "Brothers" are all good souls. My late husband Len was one. Dear Gary has always liked my soups, he eats the skin of the potatoes, we get along so well. He is a Prince.

Gary and I met in a swimming pool once years ago when we bumped into each other. At the end of the lane we stopped and chatted, that was at least seventeen years ago, we have been friends ever since. Luckily his wife Trish does not mind that I love her man. They will both visit me soon again in Texas They were here already once before the Covid pandemic placed modifications on everybody's life.

Mrs Ross. I have known hundreds of people especially many ladies, of all ages, who lived around where ever I happened to have lived...I could not write all their names . They helped me, they supported me, comforted me when they realized that I could be lonely as a girl, as a married woman, as a young mother, etc...

Mrs Ross had immigrated from England a generation before I did. She was happily married, had no children, she and her husband shared their home with her bachelor brother Cyril. He died, then Mrs Ross died and Mr Ross went back to England to end his days on the Isle of Sheppey.

Francisco LoCicero. My husband Bert helped him when I asked him to. He found him a job as soon as Francisco had arrived as an immigrant from Italy. Bert however always believed that my friend and I had had an affair, no, we never had.

We had become friends when we met, because we were the same age, had lived the same war time life, and he spoke fluent French. He and I loved panatone. He and his Dad had introduced me to this cake. We also loved to talk about our grandmothers' lives. We had lived with them, he in Italy, and I in France.

I remember when he described to me how his family lived in a camp after a bombing of 1943 when the Nazi armies were being chased up towards the North. Camp families were separated by blankets hanging from the low ceiling. He felt embarrassed when one day the blanket had moved and he saw the next door teen-aged girl's naked leg when she was lying on a cot. People in camps had little privacy. He had found a job working a s male servant in a family then had gone to work at the Fiat after the war.

Francisco married a sweet Darling schoolteacher and had a great life with numerous descendants but his health was poor when affected with cancer of the bones. Nobody knew that he called me once every year to give me his best wishes. The day I did not hear from him, I checked the obituaries of his town. I sadly learnt that my friend was gone.

Barbie and her husband Kleto Pereira. This couple and their two sons, Jason and Duncan live in England but like so many other young ones, they will always be in my heart. I had sort of helped Barbie when she was a young Indian girl who came as a lonely student to Canada and because of this close connection she became one of my surrogate children. I often hear from this young family, they used to visit me every two years but the pandemic of 2020 sort of transformed travel and visit plans for many people. If the world health improves I will see them again. If not I will wait for heaven to open the doors to us all.

Eddie B. My friend Josie's husband, Houston.
Josie never minded that I told her "I so love your husband"...there was a reason, her husband was obviously a living Saint. He was good to her,

good to his children, good to his mother in law and great with all his friends. He was a wonderful Texan, a good provider who patented one of his invention and gave a better life to all his relatives.

When he died some years ago, Josie sent me a note that said :"I know you loved my Eddie and I have to tell you he died this morning etc..."

Sue Gasiewicz & Kim Longo are two wonderful volunteer ladies who devote their entire lives to helping Veterans and many other people in need. I met them when I moved my dying husband close to the Buffalo VA hospital. Without my having asked for help, in a matter of two days they had us all settled in a house with every single items required for me to care for my Darling Leonard. My Len died of cancer 4 years ago but Sue and Kim are still in my life and as supportive as ever. Oh yes, they love their puppies, they are dog ladies too.

Clara Crawford was the first lady to sign up in my fitness class when I was hired by the NWYMCA in Houston in 1965. She was understanding of women's lives and knew how often I welcomed the support of another mother as immigrant and mother of four children. Clara would give me a dollar for each one of my children at least once a months for years and I have never forgotten how she educated me to invest so I could make my money last longer once I had been divorced and was on my own. Clara and her husband Wilbert came to Canada once to visit me and one day I received a phone call from her daughter telling me I would never meet my dear friend she had gone fo ever.

My dear friends, **Ali Kukbei, Jeannette Chevalier, Eliane Bussard** and **hundreds of other names** added to a long list in my prayer requests. How I remember all those people I loved. I could list many more. Jesus and I have a special agreement. All those dear people who have already left and those who will one day pack their bags for eternity, are and will be forever protected. Promised.

The German Prisoners
wanted to dance...

*W*e are now in June 1944, our Liberators, the worn out dearest Allies and those wonderful strong and healthy new armies of American GI's, have all of a sudden freed Normandy and all its surroundings. We, the occupied populace suddenly wonder if maybe we are dreaming.

Our radios are suddenly working, we hear the news almost clearly. In many places the town criers are giving us the good tidings, even screaming it without beating their drums.

We are free at last! Our freedom would not have been achieved without the US troupes. Our Beloved Allied soldiers and our, too often, unnoticed Underground fighters, were almost at a point of no return, those multitudes of freedom combatants were in fact, truly, totally exhausted.

This entire western part of France where I happen to claim legal status since my birth in 1930, is now free. *I am free...* However, not everybody is liberated yet. We will have almost another year to go before shouting *The War Is Over!*

The enemy soldiers are now being rounded up in our corner of the world and constrained in our very own camps. They are now our prisoners. Their arms have been removed from them. They suddenly become our very own *War Guests.*

Nevertheless, we still can see many enemy soldiers fully armed and running towards their faraway border, their home, their German mother land. We must remain extremely watchful. Those running guys now want to see their status improve and get themselves still alive back to their German homes and families...way over there. They are ready to shoot us if we try to stop them.

The problem now, for these defeated soldiers is, they have so far away to run to the East of France. A very long road ahead even if trucks carry them, picking them up as they go, on the way, while many are found running on the roads. Eventually the trucks will run out of gas. They will get ambushed by our people along the way. They remain careful and they will shoot us to make sure they keep going.

I remember two of those escaping young german men, in part uniform, bare head, half dressed and out of breath, stopping in front of me in our yard and looking at my rather small bike that I was holding next to me...They gave me a smile and said "Zu Klein" and ran away... again, towards the East.

That bike was pretty well everything I really owned in the world and I was there holding it very tight against me. I still wonder if maybe they did not want to hurt me by taking it away. Zu Klein meant *too small*. I knew that...

To them I might have looked very sad at the prospect of losing my bike. I am so sad right now recalling the state of mind I was in, but I am feeling more troubled for the desperation the two young soldiers must have felt as defeated men, while trying to run away to the safety of their own homes. I truly hope they made it.

None of these people who have stayed in French homes for 4 years would ever dare to give themselves up to their "occupation hosts", they could never trust us since we really did not really trust them either.

That is how all of a sudden in that crazy mad rush, I see our own two guests arrive, rush in our home, grab their belongings and very quickly run out without saying a word. As a young girl somehow I sort of expected they would shake hands or say something. No, they just grabbed their stuff and ran out at full speed. I saw them jump onto a passing truck that was going by rather fast but was slowing down a little when picking up escaping German soldiers on the way, as they went.

So now all those occupying German soldiers who cannot make their escape and are left behind with their hands up, are being harassed by the French people. Many of them soon realize that giving up and staying here as prisoners might after all be their safest way to survive.

Too many still prefer risking to be shot; They try to get home, they missed their families so much I guess. But within a few weeks, many are shot down as they run and I will see many German helmets, set there, motionless, on sticks and branches, standing over quickly made graves in the road side ditches. What a sad situation really!

I placed my sight and my silent soul on several of those helmets in lonely ditches. I silently prayed without anyone knowing what I was doing. On one occasion, on a country road, I came upon the grave of a German soldier next to the grave of an unknown resistance fighter. Someone had buried them next to each other and placed the German helmet on one grave and a small French tricolor flag on the other.

Poor young people, poor young men. Why did the Germans, actually those millions of them, have to trust Hitler's morbid dreams of world domination?

So at that same time, on the Eastern front, our Russian Allies are finally destroying the remnant of the German armies after that biggest WW2 battle at Stalingrad and are now pushing towards Berlin. The noose is now being drawn tighter all around.

For us all, French civilians in the west, that D-Day landing of the fresh new armies arriving from their English base, is such an unbelievable boost. It really signals to us an end to the hostilities. Finally, the enemy, those soldiers who were occupying our homes for four years, are at last, on the run.

The world has lost so many braves, on all sides, yet the war is not over. It will take almost another year.

It is ten months later, when finally in the far Northern part of where I live, the Battle of the Bulge is redefined in our favor.

On the other side of the world, the Japanese emperor accepts defeat when the second of our two atomic bombs, have made him admit that he was not a god.

... the war is finally over.

Adolf Hitler, the venerated German Fuhrer showed his so-called courage by committing suicide in a german bunker that day.

But why my title about dancing? Above...

After the war ends, a long space of time is now allowed for us all to learn of what really happened in Germany in the concentration camps and elsewhere. Everybody wants to see their families reunited. We all wait for news.

Some children born after Dad left for war had never met their dad, many little ones have sort of forgotten what Dad looks like. Some children will never see their father again, because his bones are resting in a distant unmarked foreign soil. Too often, families will wait forever, for a homecoming that will never take place.

Millions of displaced people have now to be relocated. Guilty people who expanded their powers and destroyed lives, must now be judged by war criminal courts. The world must get rid of those hateful elements legally, we must try to give a feeling of peace to the desperate left over world we now find ourselves living in.

So the months go by and in our town of La Chataigneraie the German prisoners we have kept, must work at rebuilding the roads that their tanks' slugs have destroyed. Those prisoners must also work in our fields and help our returning sickly farmers who were prisoners and worked in German factories, so undernourished.

Some of our young German prisoners have no families to return to, so many bombs have eliminated them so they will be offered to stay in France. Where else would they go?

My buddies, Rene and Andre M...neighborhood boys with whom I was picking berries for our mothers' jam making only a week ago, welcomed their father when suddenly he arrived to surprise them at their home.

Their mother, Mrs M... had cried herself to sleep often during those years. She had worked like a slave during the war, at any job she could get, even for very few francs in pay since everybody was so poor. She always said she was trying to send parcels to her dear husband, a war prisoner somewhere in Franconnie (it is a German state). The Red Cross was helping her, with sending the packages, so she was told.

Mrs M... had a difficult time raising her two boys by herself. Those sons, my good buddies, were good kids, I knew them well and they sure tried to help their Mom all the time, fetching pails of water from the well, gathering acorns for her coffee, digging dandelion plants for salads. Times were hard for us all and Mrs M never complained but hoped her hubby would make it safely back to her and her boys, from his German prison camp. She said she and her children so missed him, that husband, Robert M...

So father had suddenly arrived, kissed his family and had gone to sleep promising to talk about life the next day.

But the next day mother had found a letter on the kitchen table. Father was gone. The letter said he was very sorry but had a new wife on a German farm in Franconnie. Her name was Trudie, she was young and expecting their second child, he had to return and make a life with his other family. He had met Trudie when he was sent to work on her parents' farm and she had been nice to him. He was very lonely and had welcomed the love of a young girl his letter said.

This was a tragic happening, possibly not the only time that such bad situation happened at the end of wars. What I vividly recall is that when I spoke about it with my friends, they assured me that *they* would recover. After all, they were nine years and ten years old when father had left for the front in 1939. They, always felt that the two of them were the men of the house during the wars they said.

Their greatest concern now was their mother. The sweet wife who had waited for their unworthy father. They told me that the two of them would make her forget...I hope they did. When I tried to meet Rene and Andre M...when I visited my village in 2015, there was not a trace left of this family. Nobody knew anything about the Mrs M...mother and her two sons.

I like to think those boys took mother away for a big change, to another town or applied for immigration as I had done when I was unhappy.

Remember that a change is often better than a rest.

So now let me explain about the title above those pages...why "The German Prisoners Wanted To Dance"

When the war was finally over, we the young people asked to have dances, so our parents, friends and everybody in the village, agreed that we should get some fun some entertainment. We put on plays, organized fairs and best of all we had our dances and we could sing as much as we felt like doing. And now, the local musicians were always eager to oblige us and make us dance,

Now those recreations were held in our town hall which was the biggest spot for us to have some fun. Below that big room was the prison where the city fathers kept the 7 or 8 German prisoners locked up at the end of their working days. Of course, they were fed there, and they slept there too. I knew their guards to be some old timers from WW1 who had probably forgotten how to use a gun anyway and both were walking with difficulties with their canes. It was a job with a bit of a paycheck for Veterans who had absolutely no intention to fight or shoot at anybody.

Those two so-called guardians of our peace did not worry at all about the escapes of those fellows. They were not even locked up at night. So when the prisoners heard the music above their quarters, they turned they denim jackets that bore the huge painted prisoners of war mark on the inside out and asked to go up to watch the party.

The guards let them come up and stand in the doorway and watched for a few minutes. Having of course no money to pay the small entry fee, they sort of smiled at the old lady cashier who was standing guard at the door and she, with a smile and a lift of her chin, showed them the way to get in... I was right there, I saw her.

Now the music starts and one of the German prisoners is standing right here in front of me offering his hand for the Viennese Waltz. I accept and now the other German boys ask other French girls to dance. Everybody is happy gets along, dance, smile and is having a good time, a ball really!

Now encouraged by what they just witnessed, all those matured Hitler Yungers are dancing and having a good time...and, so are we, the girls. Our French boys understand that war lasted too long, they really do not mind and let us do our own thing. Of course we dance with all our village palls too. Many ladies just sit there against the walls smiling and watch husbands spin the young girls around also. Nobody mind, everything is feeling great.

However one lady, a friend of my mother does come to tell me that dancing with the enemy, the prisoners of War is not nice, you accept once she said then you say "no thank you". I totally ignored her counsel and followed my instinct. All of us girls did that and our own boys did not mind at all. THE WAR WAS OVER

A TRIP AROUND THE WORLD

*S*uddenly in my late forties, I feel that old father time is coming to rock and shake me; While facing the difficulties and worries that the approaching years are going to pour on my lonely bones, I feel that I should start to prepare myself for something, but I am not sure for what.

About John G, my third husband, let me remind you of the existing geographical position here, I am still near the capital, Ottawa Canada; This ex that I had remade into a bachelor again after ten months of holy matrimony, is now out of the picture, gone forever. One positive mention I could make here: at least after we had divorced I did not have his bills to pay. That task sort of faded away.

Something to mention here, I still now and then think about the man who when I felt depressed, could make me laugh with his silly jokes. We remained sort of on friendly terms after our separation. He still would call me and tell me amusing stories. I might tell you one or two later on, most stories were sort of lightly risky but moderately clean and funny. I still now silently say prayers for John G and also for his wonderful two sons and their families. I liked all those young people.

One thing is for certain now, this third and long gone husband of mine (let me say my late ex-husband, number three) does not need his hair tinted nor his nails polished where he is gone. I already spoke of John who had married me as his meal ticket...just like husband number two, Joe R. had done.

I hope you read the first issue of my Memoirs in English, "91 Years Of Love, Witnessings Of An Old Lady". You must think I was so naive, yes, you are right. The word "Stupid" is the better adjective actually. But, I have an excuse, I was so terribly lonely. I guess in my heart, I had hoped, or sort of expected, that a new truly loving husband could be found since the first one had failed me and the second one had forgotten to say he was just out of jail.

On my fortieth birthday, Bert Dworak had suddenly left me and our four children to fend for ourselves and I was not prepared for such an abandonment. Children and I needed Dad at home. We missed him terribly.

He would make such big mistakes as buying for the children, immediately after he had left, nice toys to show them that he loved them although he was gone. For example, a week after he left, he brought them a trail motorbike, something that took our children far away from my house on distant bayou trails.

So here I am now, late in the evenings and on week-ends, searching and looking all around, not finding my children. They are out somewhere with a tiny motorbike and I have no idea where they are. I am wondering..." what are they doing and with whom". All this beside my trying to figure out how I can keep paying the three mortgages on our home.

What anxiety that was at the time. One man from far away came to me one day saying that Kenny had taken a shot with his bb gun aiming to his cat and hurt the little thing. I offered to pay for the vet but all he said walking away from me: "Just look after your children and why don't you keep them home?"

How easy for people to say, I could no longer by myself keep a close watch on them. The one I needed badly was their father and he was gone.

As a family, we had always sat together for dinner at night and we had said grace, thanking God for our meals. In my silence I would daily be rejoicing at having such wonderful family, my very own, very happy little group. Anyway, this had been the situation for six months each year. I had learnt to survive the other half year trying to endure Dad's hostile and hateful evidence of his honeymoon syndrome.

At night, Bert always went to kiss his children good night. When they were little, we would sing to them. He would render to them the Brahms's lullaby that his Dad had sang for him when he was a child. Then suddenly after sixteen years of marriage, here I was the only one singing "Dodo la cocotte blanche qui pond tous les dimanches"...=- Good night little white hen who lays an egg every Sunday.

Those had been mostly happy days during those sixteen years of marriage. At least I made sure they were Happy Days. Then suddenly once more my husband had found someone else to love in the six month routine of what I described before.

Other women have suffered and felt at such a loss so I had to learn to do what they did, just learn to survive after he had assured me that it was the men's middle-age crisis for him and he would eventually be back...

I had gone to talk to Father Joe at our church and the priest had asked me again to try to cope, just wait and see what would happen. He too said that many other women in my position had learnt to keep things sewn together. My problem was that I was at the end of my line, by now my heart was broken, it could not be sewn back to one piece and I was really suffering and disappointed while watching my family life falling apart. I had to try to improve the situation. I did not really know how nor what I was going to do but I felt I had to figure out a different new way, especially that I was now without health insurance.

So for me now marriages by the number will happen in succession, one, two three...my historical accounts get very confused. My health suffers and the most difficult part of the saga is making sure my children remain happy and healthy, I must always try to keep protecting them. I am sorry to say I am not always successful at this enterprise. As one of my friendly neighbors, Mr. Baremore said to me once: "Geny, you are losing your starch".

I am speaking of time happening in the early nineteen seventieth. For you people who might remember or if you have read about those days, you might understand that those were very different and contrary times. Returning Vietnam Veterans being insulted, MLK making history, women's liberation, insurrections in many countries. All sorts of rebellions in the near East. It is not just my own world that appears tormented.

During that anguished time, I keep finding late evening hours in writing my memoirs for my children and descendants to learn about their history, in case they should become interested later on. And of course if you should like to have a laugh or two, I write these, my memoirs, for you too dear friends, the sad parts of my life and the funny portions too. My children always said my life was an open book. I wonder if they understood it all.

I know that it is often fun to make jokes about other people's mistakes isn't it! Like my having married five times, so be my guest, I allow you to have fun. Don't feel sad, my wars are over now, I do not suffer, I am happy to still be alive and enjoying my descendants, I have so many of them now. My adorable young ones.

About recounting my move to Calgary, I forgot to tell you that the ceramic factory south of Ottawa where I had found work when I rendered John G his single man status, had suddenly gone belly up and I had to find another job fast.

The purchasing British company should have stayed in Devonshire or where ever they had come from in the first place. They might have believed that making a fortune in North America would be easy. I could have told them that it was not, but nobody asked me.

So now in my almost late forties, I relocated them bones of mine in Calgary where I quickly moved. Why that city? Because I never want to be unemployed and I suddenly learnt from the news about the expending economy of that said part of the Alberta Province. It is supposedly offering unlimited job opportunities to everybody the news-people are telling us.

The news-people were right. I like to remind my children that with no diplomas in my young years I had to work at whatever I could find that gave me a paycheck. I was not choosy. Any job was good to pay the bills.

The minute I arrived there, I was pleasantly surprised, it was like an invasion suddenly in that beautiful Calgary city. Even before I had paid for the cheapest room in a downtown hotel, I was offered a job as a cook right there and then. So I grabbed it immediately, went to sleep and next morning I was cooking breakfast for the hotel guests.

In Calgary, there were all sorts of possibilities of work associated with the oil industry. You name it, you could work at it, and make a living with everything you could find, think about or invent.

While cooking and washing dishes in the new hotel-restaurant, a full time job, as I always do, I save my pennies. Then within days of my arrival I make a down payment on a very nice empty and immediately available three bedroom condo. Caroline, my youngest child is almost the only daughter in residence now at age eighteen. Kenny at nineteen is a part time family member now since you might recall in my first part Memoirs edition how I just about got myself arrested for yelling at a judge in court and telling him how to do his job. The judge, it appeared, took my advise and kept Kenny in jail for a while.

You know that we love our children no matter what, and since we blame their youth for all the mistakes they make, we should realize that we probably made some of the same mistakes ourselves before. Please, love your children dear folks, I beg of you. One day when you are old, you will realize that those descendants might be the only people in your world who really care about you! I wish my own father had loved me. I probably would never have left home.

About my buying the Calgary condo, I never purchased anything I could not afford but I always could buy a home where ever I situated myself. Bankers have always liked my financial ideas and my ways. They have always financed me with great anticipations since I always paid my bills. There is a secret to this, it is simple: you must never miss a payment on any invoice.

So now the nice newer condo is quickly furnished with second hands furnishing and a few things found on the streets on garbage days. But I must rent out a room to help with mortgage payments.

For a few weeks then I save some more and with my hard earned nest egg, I am the first person to place an offer of **five dollars** on a bankrupted coffee shop a block away from our home. Surprise! I get it. So I start my own coffee shop business. Every evening when I am about to close the door, a trustee comes to collect whatever money I made during the day and in a short time I am the unquestionable real estate proprietor of the said commercial enterprise.

Finding myself as a coffee shop owner, I have left the big cooking job of my first place of work, the hotel, I cannot handle two, I am not a magician.

In no time my own booming business is on the news but I cannot handle it for long. I need sleep and I must rest. So after four months of ownership when a newly immigrated Chinese couple offers to buy me out, I sell it to them. By then I am so tired, I sell it at a very fair price, make a fair profit, pay my taxes and am left with four thousands Canadian dollars in my palm.

From this cash I take out $2,000.00 for myself and give the rest to my children as a Xmas bonus. Since they are suddenly all grown up and out of the nest, I am now for sure alone and I truly looking for a personalized break.

I decide to do something very special. I am going to take a trip around the world, all by myself, as I always dreamt of doing when I was a very young girl. Before doing it, I start taking a good look at my whole existence.

I realize that a strange feeling of emptiness has lately surrounded me! Even while working many hours. While finding myself abruptly solitary since my children getting older have now flown away from the nest, I am suddenly getting to feel that I am becoming a senior. No!, how could that be? I am only middle aged. I just gave my last daughter away at her church wedding, in front of witnesses, how could so many years have bypassed me in such a fast time?".

'Funny, but I remember my great grand parents manifesting the unmistakable same expressions and thoughts of acknowledgment and refusal of time passing as I am doing now.

In the days of my youth, in the thirties, my great grandparents were telling me their recollections of their lives in the late eighteen fifties. Good Heaven! they were young in the late eighteen hundreds! I guess maybe after all, it is true that the more it changes, the more it remains the same!

At the time, when I was a child, I tried to understand the real meaning of those exclamations about periods of *time fast-flying* that older people always expressed. It was difficult for my young brain to understand what my ancestors really meant. The ignorance of my youth became evident with the passing of years, but of course, came a time when I really understood what the old people had meant.

So here now, alone, still in Calgary Canada. I am going to take a holiday. Why this decision? With that feeling that a cloud of loneliness is enveloping me, I am frightened of the empty silence in my home. Even today, past ninety one years of age, I still dread silence, fear the dark, mice, big storms, ghosts. The mind always carries the trauma that personal history has left on a soul. Fear is an indelible negative impression that even today I carry with that burden of my dark WW2 memory. I am sure you have similar feelings.

Many nights for me are still now, today, the mental negative events that I felt during the WW2 hostilities. The passage of years and evolving time, has not erased the terror of those vivid memories. Thinking all the time that maybe today could be my last twenty-four hours. Even if at the time, grown ups tried to keep the war happenings from the young children, we the little ones, we heard, we worried, we learnt, we feared. We witnessed the pain of so many others ...

Now alone in my Calgary condo and feeling that old sense of forsaking again, I stand up and grab snacks at my kitchen counter. Nobody sits with me at a table anymore, so, why not make it easy. A change is needed. The house feels lonely with no children, no roomers, no boarders, no husband. It feels strange and sad. Heart and home are empty.

I must no longer worry about my children, my last child just got herself a house, is now married, I know that with her credentials in early childhood education, she will never be unemployed. She does not need Mom any more. Yes, she will be a teacher. Her siblings are all well situated also at last. Now I can look after me, Mom.

My worry in those days is that the father of my children, has sort of baited them all, one by one close to him in California or where ever he is working at the time for his company. He finds them good jobs, they are tempted, they go. In the end, they all end up leaving the extremely cold Canadian weather for the Southern Paradise. First Mary, then Nancy, Kenny of course, then Caroline and her husband, now all are gone!

My pleasant and sociable Calgary boarder, Philippe, after one year of renting our spare bedroom has just moved out also, he found employment in Toronto. Ha! Another friendly face gone. He disappeared from my azimuths so the new involving events are now removing my one and only paying guest, it is sort of another negative here.

There is something very interesting for me to mention about Philippe. When a year ago he had seen the "Room For Rent" sign in my window and applied for lodging, I must have appeared reluctant and reticent to let him in my home at first.

My surprise, then shock and awe when I had answered the door, was caused by my suddenly facing someone I believed to be a drifter, a vagabond. The smiling young man with pearly teeth had very long hair, half a beard, dirty clothing, a knapsack on one shoulder, and no other belongings. He obviously carried his world with him.

When I met him in the entrance-way that late evening, I detected a pungent odor that was evidence the young man needed a bath. When he told me:"I know I look like Jesus but I play the flute"... to me the flute playing were magic words as was the mention of Jesus. Without hesitation, I had replied:"you are in! Go upstairs and have a bath, we'll have dinner in half an hour".

But now when suddenly my world appears devoid of those young crowds of loving souls in my home, although at the time still working arduously full time at the coffee shop, it is almost done there since the new owners will take over next week.

I start questioning myself. feeling that yes I need a break, sure could use more sleep too. This is almost the point of exhaustion. I do not know if I truly *deserve* it, but I might get some benefit from a vacation. I never really took a leisure time from life's daily routine, ever before. Do camping trips with four children qualifies as vacations. Do they?

It so happened that immediately after the funeral of President Kennedy this was the time when we had been moved to Houston. A big transfer for my engineer husband, hired by a company associated to the oil industry. Once settled in Houston, we could take regular holidays, and we would go camping as a family of six in the beautiful USA Rocky mountains.

We had also done it often before, in the Rocky Mountains of Canada when our children were small. We had learnt to survive the cold Edmonton Alberta but every summer, we would go on a great happy holiday. And, a few times we had done that at Christmas also since for us Christmas was just for us six. No close relatives, they were all very far away in France and in Austria.

Years ago here we were, the six of us going on holiday...the old car carrying our home made baby buggy on the roof of it. I can still see our 3 young ones sleeping piled up or all blended with blankets as best they could, on the back seat. Meanwhile, I was nursing the last one, baby Caroline, in the chauffeur's seat. I recall us calling it "our wonderful vacation" then, and to me it was a rest especially because it was a change. Now I wonder, was it really a holiday? a vacation? Probably not entirely.

There was not much luxury of physical relaxation behavior on the daily routine list for me, the mother. I recall my being almost full time cooking big meals on an open fire in blackened pots in the forests camps of British Columbia during our summer breaks.

On our camping trips, either in British Columbia of Canada or later on in beautiful warmer Colorado, our bivouacking was always pretty well ready-made of the same routine. Dad would take children walking or climbing, or play with them close by to our camping spot. He would explain to his children about the mountain climbing he used to do in Austria. As for my end, I would cook and wash dishes in creeks or rivers. I would use sand as a scrubbing powder for those blackened pots. Father was mostly involved in looking after and entertaining our children when I was cooking or doing other motherly chores. He would really try to give me a needed break.

Some years earlier, our very first outing had been with our first two children, in a borrowed pup tent, not very comfortable I assure you. And, and we did not know about mosquito repellent. We had to move quickly away during the very first night. And, to top it all, one big mistake of mine was that I had locked the keys in the car and we had to break the smallest window...bad omen! Bad start for our very first camping trip.

Later on, feeling more secured, we had purchased a big tent and a few sleeping mattresses and sleeping bags...then once moved in the US we had started with a small trailer than a bigger one. Life was improving.

One thing Bert and I had agreed upon when we had married, was that we would never burden our children with our past and our WW2 tormented years. To us this was history that had to be buried and not spoken of, nor described, to our young ones.

Now is the first time I really give them full details of the past, after having kept those memories of the past sealed in my heart for a lifetime. I know that their father told them about his own war before he died too, and, before he found himself forgetting it all with his dementia difficulties.

In those young days while we were camping, we always tried to set ourselves near water. It appeared to me that we were always very hungry in those outings of fresh air. The three daily nutrition times were not just meals, they were gargantuan repasts. One thing that I never forgot, going camping meant that my children were always famished and often in need of a thorough washing.

A nice older couple were in the spot next to us one day and the lady asked us:"why don't you come and visit us and sit around our camp fire tonight? My husband had replied:" that will be lovely but our children always want to eat. If you recall, they emptied your cookie jar last night. Would you join us instead and we shall enjoy the evening here together at our camp. That was what had been done. I had made a lot of pancakes and we had used the syrup that was locally produced. It was so good that I had purchased a case of this great natural fruit sweetener to take home with us.

Our children always appeared to have been a bit neglected, they always looked like they were starving and wore funny clothing. I know why, I was the old style seamstress, I made most of our clothes. Also I made my own and Bert's sports shirts. Once I made him undershorts with poker dot, from a cheap remnant at the store. He wore them but said he sincerely hoped that he would not get involved in an accident. Another pointer was when a kid in a camp had said to his Mom..."Oh Mom, look at the DP's" while the child was pointing at us. DP meant Displaced

Persons, those were the lost people of wars. I purchased north american made clothing more often in store basements after that remark.

A mother close to our camp one day had told me the same hunger remark about her family's being always staving, something about camping appetites I guess. She had told me:" people must think I do not feed my children, but I do". How well, we understood each other.

I remember our family doctor telling me to feed my children more. She always found them too thin. To this day I wonder why. They were rather healthy, were so active. They still are! I want to mention that our dear Doctor Ruth Asaacsen was a survivor of Dachau concentration camp.

I did not bake bread during those camping trips since I had no portable oven but I would always make lots of pancakes, crepes Suzette, popovers and similar goodies on the camp fires. Actually the popovers were not very successful. They did not pop very well as they would in the oven back at our house.

My children so loved those excursions, and outdoor meals and I must say that the memories of such camping days is still very much in my bosom, often keeping me warmer while trying to sleep on lonely nights.

So let me get back now to the trip around the world story. As a very solitary Calgarian, with everybody gone, my decision is taken. I am going to stop working for a while and make a nice long trip. When I return, maybe I should say, IF I return, if I make it back home...then, I will decide on the next step of my life. A lot of perils can watch for you to slip when you are far from home. Better always try to be watchful and keep level headed.

In those olden times, in my younger days, beside my immigration and my ten-day Ocean crossing, I had not traveled very far beside those famous family style camping trips. As long as I had small children to keep under my wings, I stayed close to home. What would have happened to our children if one day an accident would have taken us both parents?

My children's father complained one day that if he met other women on his trips away from home, it was because I never would join him on his company paid company trips. Oh yes? Try to think of what could happen to our children if we did not return home.

Well now with all of them settled on their own, I decided that I would see the pyramids of Egypt, Pakistan all the way to Kashmir and walk the Chinese wall. The astronauts can today see those sights from out of space, at the time I decided: "I am going to absorb those precious visions at a close orientation".

I wanted to get inside the pyramids and walk at least a mile on the Great wall of China. I had read about those places so many years ago when I was a child. I had my dictionary in 1939 and that was my guide, my security blanket when I was in bed early and would read, read, and read some more. Most of my youth had been under a war curfew, so reading had been my only distraction.

Now before leaving for such a big journey, I now suddenly decide to rent out my condo adding to the transaction the *option to buy*, I store stuff with friends, Caroline is still living a few blocks away from me she gets some of our furniture.

I also sell my old car. When two hitchhikers ask me if I can loan them my old jalopy, I decide to give it to them in exchange for a dollar. It needs repairs. They assure me that they are mechanically inclined so I do not worry about their future. It gives me a deep internal satisfaction knowing that I contribute to the expansion of these young men's horizon.

Those are two adventuresome city young men who want to see the world and sleep in the car or even outside... I get a thank you letter from Montreal several months later. They say they have traveled thousands of happy miles across North America with my little old car. They are now back home. Good for them! My best wishes to you boys.

Now to the WW2 Veteran connection, my good friend Reg Heywood, who never married; He is a hard working electrician, a dear friend with whom I occasionally putter around in his workshop. A Signal man in a regiment that liberated Italy in 1943, Reg happens to be this sensible bachelor fourteen years my senior.

Reg had really proposed marriage the first time we had met. Suggesting that since we get along well, as well as getting on in years, we can get old together. Why not? I have always had a soft spot for liberator-soldiers anyway. We jokingly shake on it, but wedlock must wait, just a little.

Profit from selling my coffee shop, the two thousand dollar cash Canadian money plus a few of my preserved tips will carry out my own dream. I will go around the world, all by myself.

It can be done in eighty days, I read the book, but after this expedition I must also fulfill a promise I made years ago of volunteering in favelas... two full years, no pay, but that's the other story I spoke of already in past paragraphs. Give me time, you will hear about that too.

Traveling is not really new to me. As a single girl as mentioned above, with twenty three and a half miserable winters on my head, I had crossed the Atlantic ocean in 1954, often very sea sick.

That voyage took ten days. I spent much time in a smelly narrow trough that on my ticket was called a "berth". No sheet, just a cotton blanket and a small pillow.

Mine was the cheapest, the most, the lowermost, bottom of the ship cabins. The Arosa Star had transported troupes to war twelve years before. It had not cost those Darling GI's the $600.00 I had to pay for the trip in the opposite direction, but too many had never returned to America to see their home and families again.

What sorrow! I could not at the time help but think about a sweetheart of a young man who might have laid his poor soul in this spot, my very bunk going the other way, to Europe, never to make the trip back. All this sacrifice so that I, and other young people, could live. When I think of how many soldiers never got old, it makes me so sad and I pray for them again and again in my own way.

On that famous immigration trip in the summer of 1954, my own adventurous journey, I was sailing towards new dreams, on the very same turbulent North Atlantic sea as did the Vikings, and Columbus with his three ships, and the Mayflower people and so many other daring groups. All of us were really explorers of new lands, with the same comparable goals.

Letting our bodies lay there in our bunks, the seven German girls and I had thought we would surely breathe our last. We were all seasick. The girl closest to my bed, Frieda, had lost her entire family during Dresden's incendiary bombings of 1943. Like most German girls had done after the war, these young women had first immigrated as domestics in England just like I had done.

When the violence of the sea would slow down, we could go up those stairs to the open deck to get some fresh air. There was a good live band and plenty of dancers who were eager to take us for a spin. Just think 800 men and 200 women. But when we were again in the passage way of the lower deck, and again very ill, we worried. Scared and troubled, we never spoke of the improbable Titanic possibilities since we knew we could never make it up there. But we all survived and we saw earth, Canada at last.

I must now get back to my trip around the world after finding myself as a lonely and solitary mother. Now, just as our great General Eisenhower said on D-Day to the troupes ready to leave England: "LET'S GO"...

After so many years with a great part of my life behind me, and with no more children in my home, on the loose at forty nine years of age I purchase an **open plane ticket** to go around the world, for $1,400.00 Canadian dollars. It is not feasible any more but In those days, it was an important document looking like a small ledger.

That said batch of tickets did let me get on any plane in any country. If a plane had a spot not occupied, it was for me. Any plane with a spare seat going "my way" that is. I probably could have gone in a balloon if there had been one accepting those company's passes.

With a thousand dollars in change tucked in a cloth purse on my chest, I show up at the Calgary airport with a small shoulder bag. I am wearing denim skirt, washable blouse, a sweater and a scarf. When asked where my luggage is, I say "I do not need luggage".

The agent's surprised look makes me confide to her that I have my toothbrush and a comb in my folded washable spare panties and a spare T shirt. I add that I like to travel light. So, now I am leaving to circle the globe.

Off I go, fly across the entire North American country with a few stops, then England, France, Italy, Greece, Egypt, Pakistan, China, Japan, the USA and back to Canada...I think it takes me about five weeks.

Where ever I stop, I open my eyes wide, make notes in a hand book, talk to everybody I meet if they want to chat or not. I give coins to beggars, buy a few post cards since I never owned a camera and walk a lot while observing the wonderful world around me. And what a marvelous world I am discovering!

For very little fees, I visit museums, survey peoples and customs. I try to figure out how snake charmers and magicians entertain the people with their optical illusions, I ride a camel and eat what food locals sellers cook on the street. Sleeping mostly on sidewalks, in parks or at places where it appears that people wait for buses or congregate, so I am not alone, there, among my fellow human beings, I manage to rest my bones.

A couple of times, I rent a bed in an economy hotel. In Karachi a rat found his way in my small bag to eat a tiny piece of bread I had saved. When I tell the two guys at the front desk, right away they give me another room and go hunting for the rat, Everybody was very nice and helpful. Living the way other people do in their countries has never been strange. Nothing ever feels odd to me. Moving among people does not scare me. Yet I am afraid of so many elements of life, was very scared as a child during the war but now, none of my fellow human beings can frighten me.

Somewhere in far north Pakistan, I rent a room. There is a phone next to the bed and as I am about to undress, it rings. I answer, and a male voice says: "Good evening, I saw you go in and I would be delighted if you cared to have tea with me in my room. I am just across the hallway, the door is unlocked just walk in". I reply "I will be delighted, I shall come right now" So, here I go out in the hallway.

At my door I notice that there is a young boy sitting on the floor, possibly the young son of the hotel owners. He is my personal guard for the night. He leans his back against my doorjamb. The boy points to a room a couple doors away. I walk there, open the door and a nice young man is standing at attention, waiting for me with a tea tray on a table, and two chairs.

We proceed with our friendly introductions and both very much at ease, we sit down to drink our tea. The gentleman in his mid thirties explains to me that he is a lawyer. His family lives in the center of Pakistan, he speaks Urdu and excellent English. He happens to be on his way to such and such cities to give lectures to groups of students.

I explain what my own expedition is all about and we end up talking till very late into the night. Both tired and needing our sleep, we shake hands and say goodbye and I get back to my room. The boy guard is still there and he will be still sitting there the next morning when I thank him and give him a few coins with my goodbyes.

The young lawyer is already on his way to another city I suppose and I cannot but think how wonderful it is to meet new friendly people.

I made a point of telling you this story and I do hope my friends know how most human beings are good, and friendly. We should not be afraid to communicate with them.

Something sort of funny to mention here. Years ago when my children were little, I would often tell them that they should be smart and use care, but never to be ..."afraid of your fellow human beings".

One day in later years my son asked me why I always told them not to be afraid of their "yoom and beans " I guess with my accent they knew about beans but not about the yoom...if I have to explain wit it is no longer humorous.

My journey around the world goes on I walk all over cities, visit museums again, and again. It is often cheap for me to see what other countries have in their treasured places. I crawl in Cheops' Pyramid, pay my respect to mausoleums, chat with everybody. I do not care what language people speak, I speak English or French with them. I eat dog stew in a Kashmir shack and accept an invitation for High Tea at an Iranian embassy.

I feel welcomed and share the lives of people everywhere. I just love my world and its multitudes ...all my "Yoom and Beans". A plane captain and his crew had invited me to sit in the cockpit with them. From there I admired the distant Himalayas. What a treat!

Caught in a huge rainstorm while sleeping on a park bench, I am suddenly led by a Pakistani soldier to a candle lit shelter. There, I promptly fall asleep on the ground, on a grass mat, my shoes one on top of the other as a pillow. I am surrounded by two dozen curious soldiers, all of course Muslim faithfuls. I am not afraid of anybody. The next morning I wake up and two are still there one on each side. I am offered a small breakfast that one has already gone out somewhere to get for me. I leave them with a handshake and many thank yous.

I feel safe almost everywhere. However the world is changing. I wonder if I could travel the same way now. My advise to young people who think they could do this as I did, is, *DO NOT DO IT, Take organized and safe tours.*

I walk that long mile on the Chinese Wall, suddenly realize that somebody has been following me, I notice the same man everywhere I happen to be. Never mind, I consider that he must have been sent by a higher authority to keep an eye on me. Back in Beijing, he disappeared. Thank you!

In Beijing later on, I miss my Air France plane. An arrogant French man employee accuses me of being late and refuses my entry on the plane. When I tell him I was chatting with young people, he tells me:"yes, and you probably were at the bar!". He throws back my ticket to me, turns around leaving me on the tarmac all alone.

That's when I say "you bastard will read about this one day...and this is why I am saying it to you now.

That is when the Chinese staff smiled and said "do not worry, we shall take care of you" and they did. Thank you again welcoming people of Beijing. Thanks to you I was well looked after for another two days and I stayed in a nice hotel, ate well and then was invited to fly to Tokyo on a Chinese plane. I was presented with a little Red Book, a real treasure to be found among my things by my descendants.

When I arrived in China, I had with great enthusiasm, visited the Forbidden City, got lost in Beijing, shaken hand with a skinny very old gentleman who might have survived Mao's long march. I started a conversation with him and we bowed to each other. I smiled at him, he smiled at me...He said something in Chinese, I bowed again and returned the what-ever compliment in French and in English. He smiled, I smiled and we parted.

I do that everywhere I go and meet people. Language does not matter. I make mine fit every occasion.

When in Islamabad a group of ladies offer to take me to their mosque, we wash our feet together, they cover my hair. I say my prayers with them. Arouz billahe manachiytan ira gim bismillahey etc... Something I know about La Fata.

Everywhere, immigration agents welcome me after reading the journal, the many notes I write about my Odyssey.

In Tokyo, I am refused the freedom to navigate, the immigration officers do not like to see a western woman traveling alone they say. I must go to the hotel they designate...No,no, not I! So I re-exchange the few Yens I had planned for my tour. A nice Japanese business gentleman had counseled me while flying from China and had arranged with me my complete tour.

So I turn my back on Japan, if the authorities want to restrict my visit and arrange it to their liking, I will keep on going. I am not anxious to meet Hirohito's family anyway.

I keep on flying and one day with amazement, I arrive in Los Angeles. Would you believe that to my surprise, I gained one day, like Phileas did when he went around the world in eighty days!

My own trip around the world was wonderful! Twenty five thousand miles for no more than $2500.00, so it came to be about one cent a mile, all-inclusive. What an investment!

More than a million dollars gained in my experience, enjoyment and knowledge. My universal symbol of peace and harmony was a small cross on a chain around my neck that showed I was a Christian. Yes, Jesus gave me all the protection I needed.

LOVERS

*O*ne day, on the TV news I was watching an address that a single lady was making to a crowd when she was running for some sort of election. A reporter asked her about her very private life. Was she intimate with anyone man, or may be more than one? The female politician's reply was "you can ask me all the questions you like, young man but some will just never be answered".

I thought the lady's response was brilliant. I too would say now that even if I keep very few secrets and my life appears to be an open book, I do not need to talk about my bodily functions, nor give clandestine details about the love connections I possibly have had. A private life is I think, just that, Private.

I cannot very well understand why some people enjoy sharing details about their sexuality with the whole world. Of course, that's my generation's ways. We were raised to keep reserved about FSP (Finances, Sex and Politics). We just never spoke openly about such delicate subjects.

I had five husbands in my long life, all were WW2 Veterans although the one I was married to for only a week, number two, I am not really sure. When I speak of WW2 Veterans, that should tell you right now the approximate ages of these men. All were glad at the time to find a slightly or even much younger woman to look after them.

Some rather fragile and more personal details of my life are well acknowledged in my Memoirs so if you must know information such as how I lost my virginity, you will have to spend the seventeen bucks and read the first story. Yes, I had five husbands, they were older single men. As to the Boy-Friends, or gentlemen friends, I remember them of course but there was one I truly loved and deeply mourned. All those dear people died a long time ago.

I like to believe that many people have loved me since I have always had so much love for others. So now for a change, I am passing the speech communication to a dog who loved me very much. I have had many pets but this one was my neighbor's dog, such a special friend.

I do have The Niagara Gazette's permission to use the following story, it is very similar to the one I wrote three years ago, for that newspaper. It is my eternal wish to promote pet adoption for lonely seniors.

I AM A DOG SPEAKING, I PRIDE MYSELF OF BEING VERY CLEVER:

Hello Dear Human Folks. Please allow me to introduce myself: My name is **Boo-Boo,** I am a female Pit-bull, six years old with brown and white markings. I often visit granny my old Godmother neighbor. Together we speak Canis-Familiaris, my language that for some reason, she understands very well; she is really my baby-sitter.

My human, a terrific man by the name of Roger is a first-class pet owner, calm and very patient. He feeds me very well, in fact he probably feeds me too well since last week my Veterinarian said I must lose at least five pounds.

This wonderful human of mine takes me for regular checkups although I am not crazy about his vet relationship. The other day, I quickly broke that harness when the doctor's assistant tried to give me a pedicure, then I tore and pulled off that fancy stiff collar when for some reason, she wanted to stop me from scratching. I must tell you that I am a very compliant dog, when ordered, I obey, but when I feel that I have an itch, I will scratch.

Every morning before going to his work, my dear Roger takes me to a park and lets me run like crazy with other dogs who are all under the impression that we are entering marathons. Oh! the joy, the happiness, the freedom of running at full speed with other four legged individuals! Sometimes, I pretend to take short cuts behind the bushes and trees but I am really searching for squirrels and rabbits. Of course I never catch any of them, those little beasts are somehow always much faster than I am, they disappear in ground holes or abruptly climb up in trees and tease me from above.

As you might already know, too often my relatives, meaning the other pit-bulls, have acquired a painful reputation. It is very sad because what really happened is that irresponsible individual owners of pit-bulls, have abused of our good nature. Some of my relatives have been very abused, treated most cruelly and as a result, they had to defend themselves and some dogs became aggressive.

Take my situation for instance, as a baby, somebody cut my ears short and triangular, why? I have no idea. Then somebody purchased me from a stock breeder and expected me to fight. Do I look like a fighting girl? Do I wear a wrestling belt? Of course not, but I was thrown in an enclosed sunken space to fight other pit-bulls, cousins of mine, and other large dogs. I was very scared, so I refused to fight or hurt anyone. I went to sit in a corner.

Somebody decided I was never going to be a fighter and that is when I was dispatched to the dog-pound. At least there, I found peace, I cannot really say that I found quiet because a restful place, that shelter was not. You should have heard the other dogs, whining, barking, shouting, complaining, and calling at every human walking by: "please, take me home, take me with you, I promise I'll be good"...such beggars!

People at the rescue mission were very nice to us all, they treated us well, fed us, washed our beds, talked sweetly to us, even gave us a good bubble bath once in a while. They treated us with love. All the workers were very patient with us, even with those noisy boarders wanting to speed up the adoption process by their vocalization.

I kept very quiet and perhaps because of my apparent silent good nature, I had to wait several days before being adopted. Suddenly, Roger stood in front of my cage. I saw there a handsome good man with a great soul, he looked at me, he smiled, I smiled, we said nothing but secretly I was begging him to take me home Then as he started to walk away slowly, I suddenly felt very sad. I would have cried but deep inside I was praying, yes, believe me, dogs do pray. I was begging God to let Roger hear my plea. Silently, I promised that he would never regret the decision to take me with him. I was promising that I would be a very good dog, a great companion.

Well, then very suddenly, Roger turned to me and said: "If you want to come home with me, I have a good bed ready for you, next to mine, in my comfortable house. How about it, ready? I will call you Boo-Boo".

This is how I ended up living happily with my outstanding human, my wonderful dear Roger. So now let me tell you more details about my neighbor who babysits me. She knows that my ancestry is gentle, patient and caring, I love her and she loves me too. She decided that she was going to be my godmother. I call her grandma because she is very old, and, she really seems to understand dog talk. Possibly because of her age, and having raised other dogs together with her four children while the small fry was growing up, she believes that I need training. So every day, she and I go for a long walk. What she does not appear to understand it that I am really the one training her. She did not figure this out yet, but don't tell her.

This granny is for ever promoting the benefits of keeping pets in human households. Every time somebody stops to chat with us, and trust me she makes sure people stop to chat, even if they look like they are in a hurry, I hear her deliver that same Epistle to the rest of the world.

Granny delivers that same final judgment: "if you have a pet in your home, you will not get pains in your bones, your blood pressure will go down and you will never again feel alone". To her, God must have carved this in stone when he came down from the mountain because she truly believes it and, after all, who knows, maybe she is right.

Granny has a key to my human's house. Every morning after my jaunt in the park and my wilderness excursion with Roger, she comes to get me to spend the day with her. I am never lonely there either, she cares for John. a WW2 Veteran who thinks she and I hang the moon. Those two oldies get visitors galore. These people, their friends, come from all over and keep me knee deep in treats. I feel really spoiled. Even the young lady who delivers the mail on our street gives me cookies when I run to her to say hello.

Putting aside this normal daily situation, every time my human goes to visit his sister Cynthia for a few days in New York City, I stay next door at my Godmother's house and I sleep on her bed. I have my own beautiful quilt there, it has embroidered birds of all colors on it and is very soft and comfy. I sleep well next to my old comrade and I can take all the room I need, I can stretch in every direction if I feel like expending, and she never complains.

When we get up in the morning and together, she and I are preparing breakfast in her kitchen, I am watching her every move. As I follow her and gaze at her, we chat. She says she understands everything we two talk about.

When I am with this old lady, my Granny, I try never to bark since at her age she is sort of jittery. She jumps at every noise, even when the phone rings. I do not want to give her a heart attack with my barking so I try not to frighten her, I keep rather quiet. I would feel very badly if suddenly I would make her jump and get her tripping over her own two feet. She would fall and that would not be good.

As soon as we have had our breakfast, I let her know that I am in favor of a walk around the block. The old major is still asleep anyway so we can go out for a little while. Since I want to keep the old dame alive, I want to keep her fit. Sometimes I make her jog as fast as we can run together.

The other day I saw a squirrel so close to us that I practically flew towards the silly rodent and my granny-walker took flight also. Good thing she fell on the neighbor's grass. Now she knows that when we see a squirrel, she'd better let go of that leash.

This is Boo-Boo speaking, asking our readers to please stay tune, I might soon have some more news to pass on to you dear humans. I am relating this letter today, to you from the safe corner of Granny's sofa.

Here is a picture of us taken last winter by that famous young photographer James Ness. Woof-woof...I, BOO-BOO, training my sitter.

How a boy is made into a tyrant

*M*any years after the death of my father, I hear the details of a tragedy that I should have learnt while he was alive. I could have spoken to him about this historical event and I could have understood, even possibly forgiven him for having been so mean to us, his only two children. My brother Michel's youth had also been difficult but I suppose that he, as a strong boy and a bit pampered by my mother, he was somebody who could take it. He even confirmed it to me in our later years. "*Not a real big deal for me*" he had said.

The family secret, the tragic subject matter that had been buried in my father's youth, I hear it when I am already a grandmother, from the lips of my aunt Danyele, my cousin Suzette's Mom. She must have been seven years old at the time it had happened. What I consider to have been the tragic story in my father's boyhood goes as follows...

Early in 1916, my father's mother, the powerful business woman mother of 6 children, has made a down payment on a big house with a grocery store, a promising business on the busy main street of the city of Luçon. In those days everything was paid in cash, a mortgage would be a dishonor for a family. If you did not have the money, you just did not buy.

The young family with six children has to make a better living. Raising and feeding so many young ones in the antiquated village of Grues, does not really allow them to make enough of an income for a safe future. Making Harnesses and saddles for horses and running an occasional boarding house certainly cannot keep the extended family alive and progressing for very long, even if the pack includes the still very active and working ancestors. Remember I met them all in my young years of the early thirties...

However, the close large city of Luçon is surely equipped for the better living and better schools for the children. The growing family's future is in this famous revolutionary capital of the Vendean Wars.

Luçon had been the center that had determined the Republican triumph over the Royalist fighters of Vendee, at the very end of the big French revolution. These famous Vendean Wars had taken place sixteen years after the American Revolutionary War. You may recall that one of our common American hero was Lafayette, a French hero remembered in both countries, in both Revolutions.

So now the entire household of my paternal grand parents is being moved. Finally one last trip with their last pieces of furnishings on the horse cart. My grandfather is driving the terminal cargo of goods and family from the village of Grues where that ancestral side of my family originated centuries ago. Kids are settled on top of the load.

My father, who is now almost fourteen years old, the oldest of the six children, is probably extremely tired having helped on that big move to the city for the last few days. His mother, my paternal grand mother Elise Diet (pronounced Deeyay in French) hands him her money purse and says:"keep this carefully". I suppose she might have had to nurse the last child, Suzanne, or make a change of diaper, or whatever. Today I blame her for this ducking of her responsibility.

My father, the exhausted boy Fernand, holds onto his mother's purse but falls asleep; Somehow the money bag slips and falls on the dusty road. When they arrive and disembark at the new house...everybody gets down sleepily...where is the money purse?

Now I can imagine the panic and I am sure you too can visualize the fearfulness of the situation...the cart is detached from the horse, the father of six children jumps on the horse and rides full speed back retracing the trip.

A man is encountered, he claims he did not see nor find anything on the road and keeps on walking. My grandfather makes the trip two more times and nothing is ever recovered.

So now at the new house, my grandmother calls a meeting and declares to the family: "from now on, you all are going to work like you have never done before and you Fernand (my father) will get a job and repay what you lost...I speculate that the boy got a good beating on top of a lecture. He will never attend school again.

Within a few days, after an exchange of telegrams, (That machine invented in 1800 is making the lives of people so much easier) my father is taken to the railroad station with a suitcase and shipped to one of the biggest grocery stores of Paris, The Felix Potin Company. Once a year, he will return to the family's home for a short holiday then get back to Paris to his place of work.

In Paris, his six day job a week is now driving a triporter meaning one of those three cycles with a huge box on the two wheels at the front of it. He and a few other young men are delivering groceries to customers all over the place. It is hard work, they will pedal hard while sweating in summer, freezing in winter. Now I need to remind you that the year is 1916, and we are in the middle of WW1. How could a mother have sent her child, her first born into such a dangerous place?

I need to cite that if you Google Felix Potin, you will note how important that business was in the French capital. I have discovered a picture that shows who is most likely my father sitting on his triporter on the left side of a picture. By then he is 16 or 17.

Back to the start of that business training. My paternal grandmother, had gone the day after the loss of the savings, to the encountered man's house in the village where they lived. She had found the wife acting nervously, and very disturbed apparently. The woman kept saying.. "no, my husband did not find any purse, no I am not sure that he was on that road early in the morning".

While talking in an apparently shocked nonsense, she was opening doors of cabinets pretending to look for money that she said had NOT been found. It was obvious that the husband, a poor man, had found the purse and they were not about to give it back. Times were challenging in those wartime days and you could not accuse anyone without suffering very serious consequences. Too many times, people took matters in their own hands and solved difficulties the way they considered best fitting.

...Six months later that family purchased a farm...

But now we must go back to meet my father, a boy of fourteen, working in Paris.

I remember that one day my father, although he spoke little of his youth, had told us that he had witnessed the huge convoy of Parisian taxis in WW1, transporting the French soldiers to the front to stop the advancement of the German army. This drive of taxis forcing a German army push back to their border, had been the second one of WW1 to try stopping the invasion with great difficulties.

At a time like I just described, would you have sent your child to work in a far away city so he could pay you back for the money he had lost? NO, you would not, and neither would I. But in those difficult times of yesteryear's, it was done. People had to survive anyway they could. Times were very different from what we experience or think today.

So my father, as a child of fourteen, is a kid working in Paris, full time. In the very top of the building, way up above the large store, each or the young employees has a small cubicle attic room. There they are expected to sleep, look after their laundry, care for their own company's uniform, read and stay there without burning the midnight oil. Within the huge building there is a dining room for staff. At this private dining room, the company makes sure that the young working and paid trainees-protegees are fed what did not sell at the store during the day but they eat well and almost to their content. I do not think they would be spoiled but they would have eaten enough to survive during the war.

Each month, young Fernand's paycheck and supposedly his tips, are sent to his mother. I fervently hope that he could make some of his gratuities disappear somewhere in his attic room.

This is probably what happened since between the age of fourteen and the time when he had to enter the military service, he had purchased two used musical instruments, a violin and a clarinet, had taken a few lessons, then learnt and played on his own. He also had learnt during those years, English and German by purchasing sheets of "Language self tutoring" very popular in those days.

Most people could not buy a book, they would buy loose sheets or pages ,a few at a time, from any book stand in shops or from street vendors...These bundles of a few pages were called feuilletons. You kept pages carefully and eventually would have accumulated a book in a folder held with a string or a ribbon. My parents had several in the sideboard of their bedroom.

Fortunately for my father, after a couple of lonely years, his best friend and next door neighbor of the birth village of Grues, Julien Couzinet, came to Paris and was a student at the University La Sorbonne. Later, Julien became an engineer for the City of Paris.

I spoke of Julien Couzinet in my Memoirs. I knew that gentleman rather well. We corresponded for some years too. I visited him when he was ninety nine years old.

Life in Paris went on during WW1 as I am trying to describe. I guess my father being an enterprising young boy then becoming a self made young man, he obviously successfully organized the best he could his lonely condition. I feel that he must have learnt very quickly to adjust to his new life and survive the problems presented to the Parisian population while living during hostilities. He is supposed to have had a girl friend...that is what my mother confided to me once. That is all I know.

Invasion had been avoided for the city of Paris but the enemy troupes were twice at the very doors of the capital. There were many restrictions and so much suffering all over the world, it was the first World War. Killing and suffering was affecting our entire planet.

The young boy Fernand Engerbeaud (his name had a D, mine did not)... who later became my father, had kept working, paid his debt to his mother and the family back home in Luçon, Vendee. I suspect that after possibly five, or even six years of his hard working life and the war was by then over, he could be more independent. I know that he was always poor which means that his mother still made the demands for much of the money he earned in Paris. When he married my mother he had nothing but his musical instruments and his suitcase of books made from feuilletons and his old clothing.

Years ago, his friend Julien told me that the two young fellows sometimes would meet in a restaurant on their day off and had a nice outing together talking about their very young days in their birth village of Grues.

Since the wine at the restaurant was too costly, my father would bring a small bottle of it in his pocket, purchased cheaply from his place of work with the employee discount. When the waiter had noticed, he had eliminated the butter on the table so the next time, my father had brought some butter in a small container. I am sure the young server did not expect much of a tip from those two Vendean young working men.

I would like to mention the old name of the hand made wooden butter container. It was called une coffignolle and my cousin Marie-Claire did not know that name.

Something to point out here. In the last two years of his working for Felix Potin, my father was not riding a triporter anymore, he worked often inside but he was also driving a pickup. Cars had become very popular after WW1 and businesses were doing well using automobiles instead of horse drawn carriages. My father was the very fist person in his large extended family to have obtained, I guess at age twenty, his driver's permit.

I recall how, many years ago, when for some reason he had been stopped while driving my mother and me somewhere in a city close to our home, the police man had asked to see his papers and his driver's license. I remember the man in uniform suddenly looking at him with wide opened eyes saying:"oh my, you have had it for a long time!"

When this upgrading of his working status at Felix Potin had happened, by that time, my father would have been nineteen and a half or twenty years old, WW1 was finally over and I believe this was the time when he had to do his military service. I am not sure of the exact age or duration of the commitment. Possibly two years but the military laws had changed again and again.

In France like anywhere else in the world, military service used to be voluntary, at one time it had been by drawing lots, it was so in many countries, then in France it was changed again when the Germans had shown that Germany with the encouragement of Hitler, had secretly built huge armies and all were so well equipped. The fact was certainly well proven in 1939 when they defeated us and suddenly entered France.

So with my father's starting the service and fulfilling his military allegiance, at age let's say twenty one, the year being then 1923 that is when he is now posted in Germany and is making use of the total immersion to improve his knowledge of the language.

This knowledge helped a lot I think after the German armies invaded France when I was nine and we were soon after, occupied. Our family living with two Nazi enlightened young men, had to be on its toes for four years. The fact that my father spoke German might have saved our lives during WW2.

So why was my father a tyrant and torment me the most? I was the second child, money was scarce, I was the useless girl born as the depression raged all over the world. I was extremely shy for good reason. To him there was no need of another child, I was the useless one, the sick kid. I always had a cold, a runny nose, always felt some pain somewhere, was always unhappy, not at all cute. I had convulsions often at night, suffered form intestinal worms. I did not know blue was for boys and pink for girls. It was only much later in my life that I noticed I was the only girl wearing blue stuff when my girl friends had pink clothing.

The day I was born my brother had said:"she is so ugly send her back!"

I was what you might know as the "whipping kid". When he was a young boy, my father had been abused and punished severely. Now someone else had to endure hell like he had known it. It was my turn.

I REMEMBER

To appear grown up, I had tried to smoke when I was young since I was sure it might make me look worldly. I did not like the taste and could not afford to buy cigarettes. So, I did not smoke and I am sure, I did not miss anything.

Years ago, I met a middle aged smoker who convinced me I had done the right thing. She was a bag lady. Her name was Anna. She appeared to live full time on the street, had obvious problems with hygiene and health care, her teeth were in great need of repair. I considered her a good friend of mine and every time I met her, while sitting on the sidewalk or a park bench, we shared precious time together. She would puff and puff and cough and cough her lungs out.

Perhaps a disappointment, a heart break, who knows what the factor was...Something in her brain had told her many years before to simply leave her home and family behind and change her lifestyle entirely. She was obviously an educated person, was extremely sensitive to people she met and like Diogenes, was totally in tune with the world as far as she was concerned.

Although she accepted gifts of money and other material donations, she would return the favor by re-distributing to others she considered more needy than she was. She would move about on her old bicycle carrying loads of stuff, bags , food, loaves of old bread, cookies, chocolate bars, clothing, you name it, Anna could produce it.

It maybe a strange statement but every time I shared moments with my beautiful bag lady, she always wanted to help me. I had the strangest feeling of peace and have never forgotten Anna. Although I am sort of a free thinker in many ways, I am totally convinced that my bag lady friend was an angel, a real angel. I am wondering what you think about this matter. Too many people believe that angels are real for us to ignore the facts!

My mother always said that an angel was looking after me. However, every time I got a beating I wondered where my superior defender was. I sure needed to be protected. It was no time for my angel to take a break when my father had been drinking and was going to lose his temper.

But over the years I came to believe that maybe my mother had been right, well even just a little. It made me think again.

I have always thought of my children as Golden Angels. Every week when I wrote to my mother I would tell her how wonderful my little ones were. I watched them grow then saw them make their lives their own way, for better or for worse. I always knew that one day they would be gone out of my life and I would find myself alone. I found a small poem I wrote about this feeling many years ago.

GOLDEN ANGELS

Just like Golden Angels
They fly into our lives
Spreading magic
All over the land
They bring us love and Joy
Making our world better
They work with all their might
But all too suddenly
When it is all over

They let go of our hand
And fly into the night

How true, it seems almost like yesterday that I had my first baby. There is something pleasing to recount about our first birth. Although my family life inverted to sour times many years later, on the last day of April 1956 my husband and I were eagerly waiting for the arrival of our first little bundle of joy.

We were settling down for the night in our very primitive basement room when suddenly I announced that it was time to get to the hospital. Bert, cool as a cucumber had a small case ready packed for days. He was very well organized and ready for this state of affairs. I am not sure I was. When I arrived in the driveway and got in the car, there were a few candles on the floor, a warm blanket on the back of the seat and a towel in a pail ...I do not know for what. Bert lit the candles and off we went. The old taxi had no heater and candles kept me warm until we arrived to the hospital.

THE PRICE OF PEACE IS VERY LOW

We, people of this world, recognize certainly
The cost of harmony, peace and tranquility
Is a small fee to pay
For plain serenity, yes, we all know:
"The price of peace is very low"

The rate applied to keep calm in our world
Cannot be lofty if powerless over mentality
Let's try to keep in check our eccentricity
Because, we surely know:
"The price of peace is very low"

Irritable we are when all is said and done
With faults and qualities can we survive?
Or can our world really stay alive?
Of course it can, we should all know
"The price of peace is very low"

If we cannot really think well of others
Then let's be lenient, never hurt our brothers
As an alternative to war speculation:
It is a better solution, we well know,
"The price of peace is very low"

Turning the other cheek might be a remedy
But it sure sounds most alarming,
Somewhat terrifying
With established order we know
Freedom peace is very low"

How Do I Try To Stay Fit?

My own ABC
Possibly one of my repetitions

*T*hose are only suggestions, I do certain activities without much logical thinking. If this can help, here goes: I...

a / — Add water to my routine but rarely drink from plastic bottles, glass is safer.

b / — Bake my own bread, have done it almost my entire life, not cheaper than buying, but I know for sure what goes in my stomach.

c / — Cover my mouth with a mask when I worry about germs. I take morning breaths of fresh air from outside upon waking up. It brings oxygen in my lungs and refreshes the inside of my home by opening the door.

d / — Discuss everything with myself aloud. I do this often, have always done it; I think it spooked a couple of husbands.

e / — When I envision a life without my friends, I would be terribly lonely. So I cultivate them keep in touch with them and love them all dearly the way they are. If I were to go pointing out their faultings, I would have to carry a big book for them to write down a list of my own trespasses.

f / — Fear falling, so I try never to run anywhere anymore but watch my steps because I might trip. A broken hip is not really in my upcoming plans.

g / — Gargle with mouth wash then try to sing at least once a day, even if I feel a bit blue. I have always banged on a piano or keyboard. I used carry my harmonica in my purse. I played it on a plane once but my philharmonic sharing was not appreciated. Passengers did not even stand for my Stars Spangled banner.

h / — I Hymn often small prayers because way above, someone might be listening.

i / — Insist on hugging and kissing only little dogs. I Just pat the big guys on the head. If I smile, show my teeth, the poor thing might think I am growling and bite my face. I saw it happen to a lady on TV.

j / — Just do not drive at night unless absolutely unavoidable. I do not sleep in my car ever again. If I stay over night in a motel, I should wake up alive the next morning. I got scared a few times alone in my car...

k / — Know and remember the rise of steps when going up and down stairs while listening to the clonk-clonk of my joints. Trying not to trip.

l / — Love to help others and do not refuse charity but I am not stupid either. I sent three good checks in a row to one great cause, they pestered me for many months begging for more after that. I got annoyed, took them off my list.

m /— Make sure not to judge others, they will probably want to judge me and I won't like it.

n / — Never would hank at other motorists, although at my age, you have no idea how many want to teach me how to drive.

o / recognize that phone communication is essential but I seldom use my cell. First, I really should learn how to turn it on.

P /— When I feel "aged", I want to go swimming, problem is for the last two summers I waited too long and when I got there the pool was closed for the season, that's what the sign said. I should still try to do fun fit stuff. I took in line skating at age 70, until I fell several times, then gave up. I remember a young doctor pointing at my legs and saying:"you might like to keep those two as they are".

Readers most welcomed to add to the list

BAD or GOOD HABITS

*I*n my youth, to have placed a loaf of bread up side down on the table was very bad luck. Why? Because In the Revolution days, the condemned persons would learn of their fate meaning when it was their turn to get executed with an upside down loaf of bread placed in front of their spot when they would be served their bowl of soup.

My mother, when starting a new loaf would always hold it against her chest and would make the sign of the cross with her knife on back of it. She would silently say "Thank you Lord, for our daily bread".

Something I recall and I saw it done even a few years ago when I visited my birth village; People would shake the last drop of wine or whatever they were drinking, even water, from a glass when finishing the content. It was meant to bless the earth that gave us whatever we were drinking. In Russia the drinkers would throw their glasses on the floor or in the chimney. I believe that in Russia that custom lasted a long time even after their 1917 Revolution. How do I know a lot about the Russians? Because of a good friend of ours who ran away from Moscow in 1917 when his family was being massacred. He found sanctuary in France with themany refugees hunted by the Bolsheviks . He married a lady from our village and I used to enjoy visiting them.

Before, during and after WW2, meaning as long as I can remember, my mother would take every visiting guest when they arrived at our home, for a tour of the entire house. It was a remnant of the security system of the past. This was not a feeling of showing off but you would show that there was nothing and nobody hidden that could hurt the newly arrived people. Funny but I sometimes find myself doing the same now to my guests when they arrive at my house. Habits are difficult to change. Showing people your living quarters, shaking others hands, embracing etc...all those greetings were in the olden days meant to show that the arriving person was in a safe place.

In my youth we did not have to be farmers to live like workers of the land. My grand parents having been born as I often said, with mud on their feet, had never really changed their ways. My granny never lost her peasant's accent and from the time my mother was a teenager, she was not all that proud of her origins. She adored her parents I could tell but if only they would be living more in the twentieth century like some of her friends' families, she would have been more blessed I think. I loved my ancestors old habits anyway.

As for my choices, I would have lived simply like my grandparents did for ever. As long as you had a fireplace, a garden, a few hens, rabbits, a couple of pigeons, snails and a good lock on your door, you had it made!

Those were the inheritance traits of my Celtic, Germanic, Picton, Mongolian and other ancestors that make me still look at life the way I do. If you want to have a good life, make it simple! I do mean uncomplicated. I know that you think five husbands have made my own life tangled, embroiled. Actually no, I learnt very much from all my five simple and tortuous marriages

Back in my olden days...I recall visiting country relatives whose homes were drafty and not all that comfortable but their farm animals were always very well looked after and these came first on their list of caring importance. Those animals were helping them to make a living. My ancestors always made sure that all of the little creature swere fed before the family sat for their own meals.

Perhaps you would like to know something sort of delicate. Women's underwear. I should tell you what women's panties were like when all females wore long clothing. My grandmothers and their feminine ancestors would never have worn the little bikini style panties that we girls wear today, no, that would never do!

So now imagine a pair of very loose, down to the knees pants looking like long shorts or culotte as they were really called...yes the length reaching down to your knees...The middle or the crotch is not sewn, it is left wide open. Only a few inches are actually sewn at the front and back of the waist. All women have to do is spread their legs in the bush, or crouch down if absolutely necessary. All they have to do is hold their clothing with much care to make sure nothing gets wet or dirty.

I know you will doubt my other explanation but giving birth while working in a field was also made a little easier with this sort of wear. What do you think? I can assure you that you have had ancestors, female ancestors who gave birth outside in the open field or in the bush. When babies are ready to be born, they do not usually make a sure and safe appointment with their mothers.

IT WAS THE NIGHT
BEFORE CHRISTMAS

As recounted to me this 2021 Christmas season by my friend and patient John LEY, a 97 year old Navy Veteran of Normandy.

On December 24th 1944, The USS Murphy slid up to the dock of the Boston Navy Yard in view of the USS Constitution, a fighting ship of Thomas Jefferson presidency in the first decade of the 1800's.

I was a crew member, a radio man on the USS Murphy DD603. We were just returning from the horrors of Normandy and the somewhat lesser war of Southern France and of the Mediterranean.

At the conclusion of the Southern France Liberation, my ship was assigned the life or death war against the submarine dangers still lurking for ships in support of the still raging European war.

As a tin can sailor of a ship that can be destroyed by one single torpedo, we were now assigned for antisubmarine patrol in the North Atlantic. The constant extremely rough seas made for a terrible environment week after week. The freezing waters kept the main deck constantly awash. As I would go from aft compartment, top side, forward on main flooded deck, to the radio room, my work pants and shoes would be immersed in icy salt water as I would trudged forward in to the radio room. By then, I would be wet from the knees down and would welcome the heat of my radio room work environment.

No sooner had the bos'n secured the mid-ship stern, and forward lines and gangway to secure the ship to the Boston navy yard dock, I leaped ashore, leave orders in hand to scramble for the south Boston railroad train terminal, that was just about a three hundred yards distance. Suddenly I felt that I was HOME...

"Round trip fare military rate to Joliet Illinois, return! Here take my $26.00, for coach, please!"

My itinerary called for a change to New-York Central railroad at Albany New York. Arriving in Albany around six o'clock, I realized I had not eaten anything since breakfast at 0700 hours aboard ship.

I asked a railroad employee where I could get a bite to eat on Christmas Eve. Would any restaurants be open at this time? His reply was: "No need for restaurant, all Allied military personnel can go across the street to the church basement where you all are most welcomed for a full Christmas dinner".

What a great news! That's when I literally flew across the street and found myself welcomed by the church ladies. Those Yuletide Angels were most gracious and made me feel warm all over and feeling wonderful to be back in the USA.

Here again, I could find where love was abundant as you, dear ladies, welcomed me in true Charles Dickens style. To this day I still remember you, Precious Ladies who made me feel so fortunate on such special Christmas Eve. You are still with me, today, this Christmas Eve and for ever more. Thank You again Albany NY for a lifetime of golden memories.

There were about fifty military enjoying the hospitality of Albany as served by true American people who were all making so much personal sacrifice to support the war effort.

This was an exceptional forever remembered evening as I enjoyed an hour with true Christmas celebration of LOVE instead of the hatred of war.

Signed by John LEY

WW2 Veteran of the South Pacific

*M*y Dear Leonard Reed story is another great war memorial. He was a Photographer sailor on a ship in the Pacific Ocean flying over Japanese camps and even while being shot, at he would take photographs with a huge camera attached to his body. He was lucky to have survived although at one point he had been wounded by a bullet that had gone through the fuselage of the plane avoiding killing both men the pilot and the photographer. How lucky could they be!

I have many pictures that can give you an idea of what was going on in the Japanese camps and on the Pacific front. Len spoke highly of Admiral Halsey on whose ship he served. He told me that the Admiral made the young sailors feel as though they were his sons. He wanted to protect them all my husband said.

There are not many details of LEN'S story but he described to me how one month after the attack on Pearl harbor he was one of the first groups of photographers taking pictures inside the sunken ships.

When I wanted details and asked questions, Len reluctantly said that yes the damage in Pearl Harbor was very difficult to describe. There were so many bodies reduced to a sort of jelly floating around in the ships watery grave. The floating bodies were touching the dispirited guys who were taking those pictures. He said he could never forget that scene.

Please watch for my next book called
"Leonard Reed WW2 Photographer" by Geny Heywood
Thank you. geny

13 Baker (drone aircraft)

10 Baker Under Water

Len has left me many pictures that I offered to the Navy but never received an answer so here I am using his pictures for you to see now.

30 Navy Photo Crew On USS Saidor CVE117

11 Baker (F6F(p) drone)

AN APPLE A DAY
Does it really keep the doctor away?

*Y*es, I believe it does. I often eat half a fresh apple because I know it's good for me. Since I worry about insecticides and other pollutants on fruits and vegetables skins, I peel them.

Years ago during the war, my father was a bit of a Johnny Apple Seed. Being tuberculous, too sick to be sent to the front in 1939, he took it upon himself to do his part for the war effort by getting involved in several projects. One of them was sending food to his Parisian Jewish friends of yesteryear's, all in hiding somehow.

Not necessarily the most important, but one project that I recall vividly my father speaking of, was that children who were going to be born later on, were definitely going to need a lot of fruits. So he planted seedlings of apple trees everywhere he could. Land was rather cheap I guess so he purchased a small parcel of land that nobody else wanted to buy and he started planting. Old abandoned orchard, probably thirty feet wide and a hundred long. I guess a surveyors' mistake.

Of course all of us in the family were involved in the enterprise, like it or not. Walking for miles or on bicycles loaded with shovels and water pails, we would go to that part of "The Good Earth" and work.

Since we had no way of keeping the fruit from the couple of reclaimed old trees refrigerated, all we could do then, was make preserves and of course eat much of the fruits. Came a time when we made cider with the decaying apples and yes the blemishes and the worms were involved in the making of this food product. It was a state of war, we were not finicky.

Yes, I do believe that an apple a day might very well keep me in good health...as to "the doctor away", a doctor would not come to my house nowadays anyhow.

HOW I MET PICASSO

When I said to my girl friend Jeannette that yes, I would be able to take a bus and come spend the day with her at her house on Sunday, we were bouncing with joy. I had been there once before when I had the cash. For me, in those days, to be able to buy a bus ticket to travel from downtown Nice to the village of Valauris meant selling some of my primitive art to get a small amount of cash in my pocket. A high class store owner on La Promenade Des Anglais, in NICE, had taken pity on me when he saw his manageress politely showing me the way out of the shop.

The owner had noticed my disappointment, looked at my painting on a square piece of satin, and said to his manageress " Oh yes Mademoiselle Martin, of course I shall buy it, it is charming". The lady, pinching her lips, could not help but reach for a beautiful painted taffeta skirt that someone had sold them earlier, comparing it to my miserly small piece of painted fabric. I did not care about how lovely the painted skirt was and how much a rich tourist would pay for it; all I knew is that I could now buy that bus ticket.

"We shall speak about our plans with my parents" Jeannette said when we met that afternoon at the school we both attended "they are always very supportive of our ideas". Her family had moved from Paris when her sickly artist father had taken an early retirement in sunny Provence. She and I had met a few months before while taking an esthetician course in this big city on the Mediterranean sea. I was working way up above the city, in the hills, on a chicken Farm. Jeannette and I were dreaming of starting a sort of health spa / art studio in her new home village of Valauris.

Today, looking back, I wonder how we could have been dreaming with such an aspiration when both of us were so poor. The war had been a long ordeal and although times were improving slightly, they were far from being what we might call The Good Old Days.

For some reason, the village of Valauris, in beautiful Provence, had attracted artists and communists after the war. I was just about 18, had worked on menial jobs, had been a part time telephone operator in my birth village and had daringly gone after a job that offered working every morning on a chicken farm in an area called the Vinaigrier, in the hills dominating the city of Nice.

The owner of the chicken farm was a distant friend of our family even had been my godmother in 1930. The connection making the opportunity almost acceptable by my parents. It had taken a lot of talking on my mother's part to convince my father to let me go to the other side of France. Mothers had little to say in my old Vendee,

The fear in every family was for parents to see a daughter arrive with a little bundle on her arms. I recall my father one day making an allusion that should the possibility of such an emergency happen in our home, I would be done away with, simple as that. We children were held in such regime of fear and restrain during and after the occupation that I can easily guess how the girls of my generation were not at all prepared for the real life ahead of us.

When I hear the complaints of today's youth, I scratch my head in wonder. I wish my own young years had been as carefree, exciting and full of opportunities as theirs are now.

One day, after my work at the farm while reading "Nice Matin", I had seen an ad that bragged about issuing a "diploma" to achieve a "liberal profession" when attending afternoon training to become esthetician. In truth, it was a small certificate but a paper that could be framed anyway and open a door to a hard to find job. My boss was very eager to get me that diploma. It would help me and I would be practicing my craft on her daily.

She offered to pay for it and I thought that it was a wonderful arrangement. I was working mornings, so walked for miles every day to and from the training center and was as fit as any young girl could be.

So it was that after enjoying about 6 months of the beautiful climate of Provence between work and studies, I was going to surprise my friend and took the earliest bus to Valauris.

I remember sitting next to a young girl about my age. We chatted and I learnt that she had been born in Provence and never wanted to go anywhere else. She said:" I am happy here, I never want to leave this paradise". I was thinking that I would not either if I had been fortunate to be born there.

It was still early Sunday morning when I reached Valauris, got off the bus and started walking up the hill. Nobody on the street, no barking dogs, only a fresh breeze, the chirping of birds and the smell of flowers.

Suddenly I heard a man's voice with an accent...I jumped! "bonjour mademoiselle" he said. I stopped, stared at him while shyly replying "bonjour Monsieur"...I suddenly felt like I would become paralyzed, I felt like I could faint. There he was in his full glory, his entire splendor, only a few feet away from me, same age as my maternal grandpa, The GREAT PICASSO!

Here I was, facing the greatest artist the world has ever known, the revolutionary, the great visionary, the great lover, the breaker of hearts. Newspapers were full of him every day. Somehow he was a bit shorter than I imagined him to be, here he was, facing me, his glaring eyes were burning through my entire being, like devouring me, and I, almost paralyzed with shock was desperately trying to put my brain back in focus.

The GREAT PABLO was standing among the flowers and the green-eries of Provence, in his underwear, yes, in his underwear! I had never seen even my own father undressed, not even when the family went fishing for shrimps in the Atlantic ocean. But the great Picasso's beautiful body was tanned to perfection. The man who used to boast that he was NOT A GENTLEMAN was barefoot, his almost bald head uncovered, he was holding a cup He held no cigarette in his hand contrary to the numerous newspapers' photographs. I noticed the absence of cigarette but please do not expect me to tell you the color of his underwear or the size of the cup. I was totally smitten with emotions, was I maybe falling in love? needless to say I was still a virgin.

Absolutely overcome with surprise, shyness and a sort of fear all wrapped in one that after that exchange of greeting and a reply to the trivial statements about the weather, I found myself hurrying away. Yes, stupid me, I hurried away, my face red as a tomato, my heart pounding in my chest, my whole being shaken with embarrassment. I thought I would faint. The look in Picasso's eyes is not a vision you can easily forget.

When I arrived at my friends' house I told Jeannette and her parents about my encounter with the famous artist. "Oh yes they replied, he is very involved with ceramics right now and the people say that he has just moved here with his young family, his presence will be a shot in the arm for Valauris…". Of course history has told us that it was. Picasso did place the old Roman village on the map. I think it was Francoise Gilot, his most famous muse, his companion, his model, his wife at the time, the mother of two of his children, was actually the better artist of the two. He painted her in very unflattering displays of emotion and destroyed their relationship. How sad.

The next day, I reflected on my meeting with Picasso and of course asked myself why I had not calmed my nerves down and made a proper connection, it would have been easy. I had been just too shy. My art would certainly have been better than it became and I might have been able to make a living from it. I liked ceramics and the mysteries of clays and glazes. I so loved the arts.

I made the mistake of writing to my parents that I had met Picasso, the reply was an order from my father, I was to return home immediately. There was no choice. Once again I was under his tutelage and stayed that way till December 1951 when I went to work as a nanny in England, free at last.

Reminiscing...

There is a public library in my birth village today but it was not there in my youth. You could buy books from a very tiny store. Prices were out of reach for children with no medium of exchange. My brother and I trusted that our maternal grand parents' new years traditional small money gifts would help us to buy a book. They, in turn, for their own reading, trusted one only publication, their farmer's almanac.

In my youth, people shared daily newspapers, splitting the cost and the chore of going to the store to buy it. You would take turn every week. I remember my grandpa walking to the tobacco shop and bringing the daily reading, then studying it with Grandma from first to last page. I would sit between them on a small chair and listen to their comments. Then he would cross the street and hand it to the neighbor that same day. News had to be fresh, not next day news. The following week, it was the neighbor's turn. The young son in that house was Pierre Chauvet, a boy I trusted to be an intellectual. He was an only child. I remember his getting get his BA at age 18 and he became a great teacher.

Newspapers were not wasted nor lying around since after being read and re-read, they ended up to be utilized in the half moons.

On new years day, my grand parents would ceremoniously present us an envelope containing a few francs to place on a savings book that my mother managed for us. That is how after a few years I purchased my Larousse dictionary before the war in 1939

Let us speak about health. Since having eaten various plants, root-stock and questionable organisms for almost a century, I am now baffled about which substances might have contributed to keeping me active and healthy for so long.

Was it onion, garlic, apples, stewed nettle or purple clover? Perhaps my dandelion salads, wild mint, the amaranth that grows abundantly in ditches. It could just be apple seeds, or, the almonds I find in the stones of certain fruits when I crack them with a hammer. I have always chewed these edibles with enthusiasm even if people claims they are toxic. I am now almost convinced that it protected me against malignant afflictions since I count a great number of cancerous departed relatives. I might have done something right after all?

Is it possible that the very same nutrients did try to kill me and my body fought back? I cannot tell you for sure what kept the reaper away from my door until now.

Perhaps the benefits or detriments derived from such variety contributes to a proper balance for vigor and survival. I am willing to donate my corpse for study. Do not rush with this task, I have many unfinished projects yet to realize.

Regarding foods that appear in the news as lifesavers one day and homicidal the next, my ancestors would simply have unheeded the counsel. Roman emperors protected themselves from being poisoned by absorbing small amounts of toxic matter so that their body would sort of immune itself. Perhaps I have been doing the same without realizing the fact.

I often wonder if maybe the allergy problems that are so prevalent today, are not possibly due to the early avoidance of toxins from the bodies of young children. As a child, I ate the same foods that the grownups around me had on their plates. I have never had an allergy.

I remember at two years of age, a family friend Edmond Ouvrard, bringing me a small bag of peanuts in the shell. I was just going for a nap. How I loved the treat. I wanted him to visit often if he were to bring me such goodies! I could only securely tear open a couple of them with my teeth. I remember falling asleep and finding the lovely peanuts and the shells all over my crib upon waking.

About allergies, I must jump out of my youth into that of my four children who drunk spinach juice in their baby bottles from day one. I also poured broth with milk in their baby bottles and never worried about hypersensitivity. Our cat might have been responsible for some sniffles and runny noses. That was long ago, my descendants are all fit and healthy. Well, the ones who survived that is. My family, like yours, experienced its own tragedies.

How You Can Cure Your Loneliness...
YES, YOU CAN!

The canadian government, in dire need of women after WW2, had offered me while I worked as a maid in England, an assisted immigration domestic job visa that I had accepted immediately.

We cannot expect much from our families anyway, they are way over there across the Atlantic Ocean. They cannot do much to help us.

Every month we are sending fifty dollars to Bert's Mother. My then, never met mother in law, is a widow trying to keep her eighteen year old last child Gerhard, in university. She also receives some assistance from her oldest daughter, a journalist who lives close to her in Vienna.

Her second child is her oldest *engineer* son, Bert Dworak, my husband, now working in Canada. He is not asked to send anything to help mother. He just never tells the family in Austria that he is not recognized as engineer in his new country, Canada.

Bert actually works at whatever he can find that gives him a paycheck. Naturally he wants to help his family. So no matter how hard it is for us, we just send those fifty dollars every month.

And here we are now, a new and young family, the typical new immigrant or displaced people unit, we just try to hold out through the cold northern winter. We are just waiting for better days ahead. Now living where jobs are plentiful for us all immigrants, even if the work is poorly paid, we are very thankful. We are working.

We are always cold, very cold, having too few warm pieces of clothing. But we feel blessed and we dream of a good future in Edmonton Alberta.

Canadian winter is not much to sing about, thirty two below, for several months of a year, but we do have work and money comes eventually in our palms. Hold it now, stop just for a minute...do you realize what 32 degrees below zero is? Impossible! Even today, now I have a hard time thinking it was ever possible for me to endure.

So, here I am now, the year is 1956, a brand new mother of a tiny infant and I am already expecting a second child; My health is certainly not the best, we hardly have enough money to feed ourselves and no relatives to turn to since our relations are all in Europe. Bert and I had agreed not to wait much longer to have children but I did not expect to suddenly become a baby machine. Anyway we must face our life as a family now we are no longer just a couple.

So, as to our working situation, after leaving the glass factory job of Toronto, my husband is employed as a mechanic as soon as we arrive in Edmonton. I am right away hired cleaning rooms in a big hotel, The Mac Donald. The extraordinary advantage for me is, well at least for the few months during which I am working there, free meals.

Thanks to the hotel management, we, the poor employees, are served a good meal every day before going home. You should have seen all our plates, clean as whistles when we had finished our meals.

I remember my very first great good dinner served to me at that hotel staff dining room: a beautiful fried slice of beef liver, with fried onions, scoops of mashed potatoes and peas. This is the first time in my life I see someone serving mashed potatoes with an ice cream scoop! Some good brown gravy on top of it all, and as much of it with bread and butter I wanted to eat. A real feast!

What a banquet for starving immigrants! I cannot forget how good it is. And the fact that I can ask for more and not be refused is such a great sustenance for me, for all of us employees since we are all mostly the newly arrived workers from depressed Europe, what a banquet!

In addition to the room cleaning job, by helping a couple of French waiters I met working at the restaurant part of the hotel, I gather a good plate of left over food to take home to my husband. All is well for these few last weeks, until suddenly I find myself so sick I cannot work. I am pregnant.

This is when I have to take *early retirement* to care for the baby on the way, and of course make sure I can survive. I end up two weeks in hospital, I am supposedly too underweight to be a mother. We must improve our living conditions said the medics. I suffer from malnutrition. Little by little we will have to pay for those two weeks of rest and care in the hospital bed. Health Insurance has not kicked in yet. But we shall make it. We shall survive.

So now finally, Bert finds a better job, than another better yet. We can see a bit more money and we can see a bit of light at the end of the tunnel even with a first baby in our arms. We move in a little shack that we purchase. It offers us three mortgages but who cares. We move in our own house with our very first baby Mary. Our move in is easy, we hardly own anything. A bed and a tiny crib.

Once in our own house, now my health should get better, I now will be able to do all sorts of work, babysitting, sewing, laundry, tutoring French to several students, but while nursing our first child, suddenly, I am sick again, pregnant again.

Life is suddenly too depressing, I need help. Bert has enough to do bringing the paychecks to keep us all alive and within twelve months we shall have two children to care for besides our own skinny bodies.

Before going further, here I want to show you our wedding picture October 15/ 1955, not much of a ceremony, the landlady, who had rented us a basement room for a while before our marriage and family life's beginning, took our picture. I love that photo. I am almost three months pregnant with our first baby, we are happy. My wedding present from Bert, the suede fringed Indian jacket I am wearing, my gift to him is a Boulova watch. His very first wrist watch. He will wear it for sixteen years.

I survive long sickly days with a baby who needs milk that I do not seem to produce, Mary cries a lot, I feel so tired and lonely. I do not really know anybody in our neighborhood around our own ran down small house, I feel so alone with nobody to talk to or call on for help. Oh and BTW let me tell you that yes, you can get pregnant while you are nursing.

Feeling extremely depressed and suddenly very lost, I decide one morning to go knock on a neighbor's door as soon as my husband is gone to work. I had bumped into that older couple in the lane way, shortly before, only once, when we first moved in the house. They lived behind us and we had exchanged just a few words.

Here I am suddenly hesitantly knocking at that entrance, the lady answers and opens the door. All I can do is murmur a greeting and start crying. Mrs Ross, a lady who is fighting a harder battle than mine since I learn later that she is dying of cancer, immediately evaluates the situation.

Mrs Ross walks with me across the lane back to our house where I have my baby crying to be fed. The lady sits with me and starts asking me questions. When I apologize for bothering her, she says the sentence I shall never forget..."*But that's what we neighbors are here for, we are here to help you, remember that*".

Can you imagine? This was sixty four years ago and I remember this phrase as though it was being said to me only this morning.

As you are reading this right now, can you recall a moment in your life when you felt that same way, lonely, sad, dejected, depressed and with that same feeling, that same total mental state as I just described? I bet you can recall finding yourself in the very same situation. My faith had silently supported me in such fixes of course for years but that morning there was just no way out of the slump for me.

In no time this dear neighbor realizes that mine is a family in distress, afraid and ashamed to ask for help, she passes the word all around, within a few hours all the ladies in the neighborhood houses come to reassure me. From now on, everybody makes sure I am all right, we get warmth, support, visits, food, toys, clothing, furniture.

When spring comes, I get help to get my garden started, get my own veggies growing. We have summer tea parties in our backyards watching our children play together. We meet for sewing bees, social gatherings, I am living abundant happy times.

Mrs Ross loses her battle to cancer a few months after we met. From her I learnt what a wonderful great life you can give yourself and the rest of the world if you talk to neighbors, chat with people all around even if you never met them before.

I do that all the time. I chat with everybody, I never feel lonely. I communicate with just about all my fellow human beings. This is my remedy to loneliness. I love people of the world entirely and unconditionally. Trust me, this is the true remedy to loneliness. It works.

THE END OF THE SEQUEL
WITH LUCKY ROOSTER

My Celtic ancestry side has always placed their Gallo as a specially lucky fowl. This is one of my own Picasso style paintings, I call this bird, "The Lucky Rooster". If you take a few minutes to study it, then make a quick sketch of this bird on a piece of paper, you could be surprised. Something fortunate might happen to you right after you make the design, several people have told me in the past that it brought them luck. I am not superstitious but it might work, if it does, it's worth a trial. Go ahead. Anything for good luck!

Here I am at the end of a sequel that covered many subjects. I like to remember that as my publisher mentioned: *Our life has to be truly cherished with every breath we take.* So I wish you all the very best.

Thank you, Geny

Romans 5:8-10 ESV
[8] but God shows his love for us in that while we were still sinners, Christ died for us. [9] Since, therefore, we have now been justified by his blood, much more shall we be saved by him from the wrath of God. [10] For if while we were enemies we were reconciled to God by the death of his Son, much more, now that we are reconciled, shall we be saved by his life.

Romans 8:38-39 ESV
[38] For I am sure that neither death nor life, nor angels nor rulers, nor things present nor things to come, nor powers, [39] nor height nor depth, nor anything else in all creation, will be able to separate us from the love of God in Christ Jesus our Lord.

James 1:27 ESV
[27] Religion that is pure and undefiled before God the Father is this: to visit orphans and widows in their affliction, and to keep oneself unstained from the world.

Jeremiah 29:11-13 ESV
[11] For I know the plans I have for you, declares the LORD, plans for welfare and not for evil, to give you a future and a hope. [12] Then you will call upon me and come and pray to me, and I will hear you. [13] You will seek me and find me, when you seek me with all your heart.

Thank you to all working people during pandemic.

PLEASE RESPECT YOUR CHILDREN

*A*t age nine, I was a free companion to a senior. When a friend of ours died at age 78, his widow was left alone and I was ordered to go sleep with the old lady.

Each evening, I'd carry the breakfast that my mom had packed, a small bottle of chicory with milk, and a piece of bread in a bag. The next morning I would gulp down the cold drink after having eaten the bread. I'd then get myself to school.

My being given the spot where the corpse had laid was not a cheerful experience sleeping between sheets that smelled of naphthalene.

If anyone had asked me if I wanted to be a companion at such a tender age, I would have declined, so I was given a volunteer job I did not want, nor liked, from October to Easter.

Add to this stressful situation, the torment of war that everybody around me talked about. Then my 9th birthday had passed but was not even mentioned. I do not really feel sorry for myself but I want to point out to parents:

PLEASE respect your children.

LIST OF CHILDREN'S STORIES
AND SONGS BY GENY HEYWOOD:

A / The PROTO series:

#1: **PROTO**, What do You Do When A Dinosaur Is Born In Your Garden?
—-Available in English, French and Spanish / Published by AuthorHouse in America
#2: **TIRANO**, Another Dinosaur Is Born
—-Available in English / Published by Author-House
#3: **STEGOTA**...The Great
—-Available in English / Published by Author-House

B / Christmas Story

#1 **CANDY, The Turkey Who Missed Christmas**
—-Available in English / Published by AuthorHouse
#2 **CANDY, La Dindonne Qui Manqua Noel**
—- Available in French / Published by EDILIVRE A PARIS

C / Teaching Children About Death

I Am An Amazing Child
—-Available in English / Published by EDILIVRE A PARIS

D / History (CHARLEMAGNE)

—-Available in French / Published by EDILIVRE A PARIS
A didactic poem

E / JEUNES ARTISTES DE VENDEE
Samples of children's art work done at my 5 day art show in France
(Promoted by SUPER U company) Published by EdilivreAParis

F / Grandma's Fitness For All Ages.........ready to publish

G / History of the world, a long poem in three parts ....ready
to publish

"Memoires d'une Vendeenne, Temoignage d'une vieille femme"
Memoirs published in France by Edilivre already on the market
for 2 years.

List of my SONGS
(Lyrics by me but I own rights to the music since I paid musicians of
Nashville to write the music and sing the songs)

CANDY THE TURKEY WHO MISSED CHRISTMAS \
I wrote the lyrics and paid a singer to write the music and sing it...
It is the song number 7 on a disk called Rising Christmas Star by
Paramountsong.com. I can send it by attachment I have several others
but will have to find them.

Books Published with Xulon Press

  1–**Ninety One Years of Love**, Witnessings of an Old Lady
  2- **GREATEST ARTISTS**, A creative experience for YOU And
    ARTISTS OF ALL AGES
  3–**92 Years of Love**, Witnessing of an old lady" The Sequel

CPSIA information can be obtained
at www.ICGtesting.com
Printed in the USA
LVHW031804040322
712646LV00009B/800